Pizza

& the Art

of

Life

Management

Also by Maura Beatty

Bootstrap Words (Pull Yourself Up!)

Kendall/Hunt Publishing Company

Stress Arresters Video

Alpha Beatty Communications/
South Texas Public Broadcasting System

Pizza
& the Art
of
Life
Management

Maura Beatty

KENDALL/HUNT PUBLISHING COMPANY
4050 Westmark Drive   Dubuque, Iowa 52002

Cover Design and Illustrations by Chuck Beatty

Back Cover Photo: From the video *Stress Arresters*, produced by Alpha Beatty Communications and the South Texas Public Broadcasting System.

Photo on page 217 by Greer Evans

Book Design by Chuck and Maura Beatty

Text Edited by Nancy Mark

Published by Kendall/Hunt Publishing Company

Copyright © 1996 by Alpha Beatty Communications

Library of Congress Catalog Card Number: 96-75806

ISBN 0-7872-2142-2

Printed in the United States of America
10 9 8 7 6 5 4 3 2 1

For Maggie and Al Beatty,
Mom and Dad,

Your love and support inspires me
to ever greater heights…

For Beth Alden, my sister,

You make me "wicked proud,"

&

For Charlie B., my darlin',

You're my super supremo!

Table of Contents

Prologue

This is a book about stress management.

More than that, it's a book about taking care of yourself in such a way that you can actually decrease the negative effects of stressful circumstances in your life.

If you picked this book, you probably have a great fondness for pizza, as I do. You might be wondering what pizza has to do with stress management, or life management, for that matter.

The answer is simple, really.

Practicing my *Stress Arresters* program is a lot like eating pizza. No matter how much pizza you choose to eat at any given time, you always have to eat it one bite at a time. (Even if you take big bites.)

No matter how much stress you may currently be experiencing, you have to handle it a "bite" at a time, too.

If you don't handle it this way, you'll get the same kind of results you'd get if you tried to stuff an entire pizza in your mouth at once. Attempting to "bite off" (translate: deal with) too much stress at one time will choke you.

Everyone who loves to eat pizza has a combination of toppings that is their personal favorite. Some people love the pepperoni, lots of onions and mushrooms, or Italian sausage and sweet peppers. There are even people who love tomato, onion and pineapple on their pizza. Some people pile on the anchovies, while others go the route of smoked chicken and goat cheese.

Eating pizza is a very personal activity, which makes it a lot like reading this book.

There is no right way to read it—it's just a matter of personal choice. And just because you read it once doesn't mean you won't want to read it again. And again.

When you eat pizza, do you pull the pepperoni off of the cheese? Do you eat the crust right away, or save it for later?

Whatever you do, you're still making personal choices. Just like you can when you read this book.

You can read each of the sections in order, you can skim the highlights of each section, or you can jump in at the middle and maneuver towards either the back or the front.

Each section addresses one piece of the whole "pizza." Pick the one that interests you, and dig in.

Part One contains general information about stress, how stress affects your brain, the specific physical effects of the stress response, and the "chains" section. The "chains" section is where we discuss the nitty gritty details of how we, personally, get to be so stressed. There are also some workpages to help you to identify your own particular "chains."

Part Two contains information on the process of doing things "a bite at a time" in the Four Week Plan. The Four Week Plan is the process of changing one thing a week for four weeks, so you can start to increase your physical ability to withstand the effects of stressful situations. This section also contains information about affirmations, how they work, and how you can use the affirmations that you will find throughout this book. There's room for you to create your own affirmations, too. There are exercises and workpages to help you track your progress.

Part Three contains the Four T's, four specific strategies for combatting the mental effects of stressful circumstances. There are exercises and workpages to help you track your progress here, too.

Part Four is the Epilogue. That's the place where it all comes together so you can get an idea of how the entire process will work in your life. You will have gotten the details in the previous sections; this is the place where you can get the "big picture."

Part Five contains the Extra Toppings: extra details on topics in which you might be interested. These little extras are part of my longer *Stress Arresters* workshops, and were not included in the PBS *Stress Arresters* video.

At the end of the book, you'll find a list of Resources, divided by topic. You might find them useful in expanding your knowledge of the information presented in this book.

So enjoy yourself. Make a meal of it, or just have a snack. Whatever you do, I invite you to make this process your own, and to share with others the parts that are useful to you.

Like pizza, all good "food for thought" tastes better if it's shared.

Bon Appetit!

Maura Beatty
Austin, Texas
Valentine's Day, 1996

Acknowledgments

No project is ever a solitary effort. This one is the result of the work and inspiration of many people over nine years.

It's important to say thank you for all great gifts. Each one of these people has been a great gift to me.

First of all, Scott Allen, MA, MBA, who asked the original question. Thank you!

All the people who came to those early stress management workshops at Charter Hospital, who were an inspiration to me even then. Thank you so much for teaching me, and learning with me.

Mike Harrison, who coined the term *Stress Arresters*. He helped me when I had to come up with an alternative to *Stress Busters*, which I'd been using for three years. It turns out the name was also being used by a massage parlor.

All my audiences in my *Stress Arresters* workshops and presentations across the country, who cheered me on and told me how the strategies worked for them. Thank you for sharing the journey!

The folks at KEDT, South Texas Public Broadcasting System, for believing in *Stress Arresters* and helping to make my dream of a national video a reality: Jeff Felts, our producer, who championed the video and relentlessly pursued it; Adrian Arredondo, our director, whose brilliant editing transformed our work into art; Peter Frid, the General Manager, who gave it the thumbs up, and Don Dunlap, Assistant General Manager, who coordinates the distribution of the *Stress Arresters* video and takes care of the details. All our friends and supporters at the station, who came to the rehearsals and the taping, and who always make sure we have doughnuts & pizza for the pledge drives: Myra Lombardo, Karen Graham, Diana Hollingshead and Andy Cook. Thank you all!

Mary Helen Anderson, my dear friend and ardent supporter, who came to every single *Stress Arresters* rehearsal *and* the taping. She responded to every punch line as if she was seeing it for the very first time; her laughter and energy transformed even the hardest work into play. Thank you, my dear! You did it, you did it well, and you looked good doing it, too! I love you.

All the folks who gave of their talent and love for the *Stress Arresters* project: Shirley Markley, my skilled video coach and our voice-over genius; Tim and Sandi Thomson, who offered technical advice on the video, as well as making all of the artwork and illustrations possible by supplying techno-magic at just the right moment; Roger and Karen Powe, who believed so much in the project that they became a part of it, all the while making sure I looked great for the cameras; all the folks who came to the practice presentations, so I could recreate *Stress Arresters* for video; all the folks who came to the evening rehearsal tapings after working all day; all the folks who came to the Saturday taping and stayed all day. Thank you, every one of you, for making such a difference for me on this project!

My editors: Nancy Mark, my Minnesota nonpareil and chief editor, whose sharp mind and thoughtful comments kept the endless rewrites entertaining. My associate editors, Ben Tetzlaff, Al Beatty, and Chuck Beatty, jewels all, whose insightful comments and eye for detail helped me to shape the rough edges into something finer. And finally, my ever-patient editors at Kendall/Hunt, for agreeing to all the extensions with gracious good humor. Thank you, each one of you!

My family, a treasure beyond belief. Some of them are related by blood, some by choice. Every one of them has made an immense difference in my life. As a result, my relationship with each one of them has had a direct effect on the writing of this book:

My mother, M. Eileen Connolly Drennen, a great teacher, supporter and nurturer, whose ability to withstand the slings and arrows of outrageous fortune with poise and grace, a great sense of humor and a joy for living, has been an inspiration to me all of my life. I love you, Ma, and I thank you.

My father, Dr. D. A. Drennen, from whom I inherited a talent for writing and speaking and teaching. Thanks, Dad. I love you.

Al and Maggie Beatty, whose love and support make all things possible, and whose belief in this work makes my heart soar. I could not love you more if you were my own parents, Mom and Dad, and I thank you.

My sisters and brother, Deirdre, Susan, Eileen, Don and Beth, and their families, who are such a big part of my life. Individually, and as a group, they continue to inspire me to reach for the stars. I love you all, and I'm so proud to be your sister. Thank you!

Scott & Beth Beatty, who have taken me into their hearts and their home as a sister (soon to be an aunt!) and who always leave a light on for us weary travellers. I love you both, thank you!

Maggie Veigl, my dearest friend, and adopted sister, who constantly reminded me that *Stress Arresters* should be a book. For over fourteen years, through thick and thin and everything in between, she's been a Light in my life. We certainly learned a lot about stress together! I love you. Thank you, always, for everything.

My darling Jakobh and Jenni Coleman Veigl, children of

my heart, who are growing up faster than I can imagine, who make me proud to be their fairy godmother. I love you two cherubs! Thank you for the Light you bring to my life.

Greg Veigl, my new brother, the love of Maggie's life and the "daddy" to her children. Thank you for the Light you bring to the people I love! I love you!

George Earl Gochenaur, my "fairy godfather" and Rhea Byers, my dear friend and adopted sister, who have known me for over twenty years, who loved me when I didn't love myself, and who I am proud to call family of my heart. I love you both, and I thank you!

And my partner in all things, my heart's inspiration, the Vice President of Details of the Universe: Chuck Beatty. Without him, without his love and encouragement, without his exceptional talent, this project could be only half of what it has become. I thank God every day for the gift of this man in my life. I love you, Charlie, and I thank you!

Finally, I thank you, dear reader. You have chosen this book. You give me the gift of the opportunity to speak from my heart about all that I have learned along the way. You are a treasure. Spread your Light in this world, and celebrate your glorious self!

Pizza

& the Art

of

Life

Management

Introduction

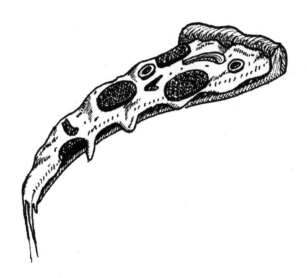

The Creation of *Stress Arresters*

Stress Arresters is the name of my stress management program. It's the title of the PBS video for which this book is the companion volume. And it has been the vehicle of much of my professional success for the past nine years.

For something which has become such an important part of my life, it started out quite simply in the fall of 1987.

In August, I completed my tour of duty in the United States Navy after over 11 years of service. Then, because I was a Navy-trained substance abuse counselor with an honorable discharge, I was immediately hired by a the largest psychiatric and addictions hospital in Corpus Christi, Texas.

Everything else, as they say, is history. Although nothing I planned worked out as I expected.

When I first started my new civilian job, I was pretty pleased with myself. I had managed to get enough of the right kind of training in the Navy to be able to find an excellent job in my field right away. I was excited about my new life and ready to start building a successful future.

Unfortunately, I hadn't taken the differences in military life and "civilian" life into consideration.

By September, after 30 days as a civilian, I was still in culture shock. I felt like I had landed on a planet in some distant galaxy and was only pretending to be a native. I practiced nonchalance and acted confident, even though I didn't feel either. To complicate matters, my marriage was on the rocks, my mother-in-law was dying of cancer, and I had absolutely no idea of how to do my job.

In retrospect, it occurs to me that there are two kinds of workplaces in the world. One kind of place has specific procedures for the way things should be done, and every employee's first task is to learn those procedures before he or she actually starts doing the job.

The Navy is like that, and so is Catholic school. Those

were the two places I'd gotten most of my education about the world. I expected procedures, even though I was usually the person who was always trying to color outside the lines. At least I knew where the lines were!

The hospital was one of those other kinds of places. They hire you because they think you're smart enough to know what to do. The administrators consider you capable of figuring out the necessary procedures without any coaching from them. It was a great compliment, and I took it as such. However, after all that time in the military, and with my parochial school education, I was completely out of my element.

I was fearless, though. And I was trying desperately not to look clueless.

During my first few weeks on the job, I took one of those self scoring stress tests. You know, the ones where you assign points to the various changes you are experiencing, in order to assess your level of danger from overload. When I added up my totals, my scores were four times as high as the highest stress combination listed. That's right, the one which indicates that you're a sure candidate for a cerebral hemorrhage or a coronary bypass.

Despite those scores, and my present set of circumstances, I managed to stay calm enough to fool everybody into believing that I was one of those people who led a charmed life. It was here, in my first few months as a civilian in my new job at Charter Hospital, that I became convinced that there is some beauty in the strategy of "fake it till you make it."

One day in early October, Scott Allen, a co-worker, came into my office. He asked me if I could put together an hour-long program on stress. (I guess he had me pegged as some sort of expert.)

With my usual bravado, I gallantly agreed to help him. "No problem," I said. "Piece of cake! Leave the details to me." I certainly reduced *his* stress.

As soon as he left, I shut the door. It was only then that I checked with *myself.* What was I going to do? I'd never actually written a program before.

Sure, I'd presented training programs in the course of my career in the Navy, but I'd never actually written one. I had attended lots of workshops and seminars over the years, but I had no training in instructional design. For all intents and purposes, my goose was thoroughly cooked.

Never one to be put off by circumstances, I assumed my creative position. That is, I sat on the floor of my office and kicked off my shoes. (Sitting on the floor like a pre-schooler is a great position to take when you have absolutely no idea of what you're doing.)

My mind was as blank as an empty TV screen. After a short time, an image appeared. It was Jacob Marley, Ebenezer Scrooge's ill-fated partner, from Dickens' *A Christmas Carol.* The image was in black and white, just like in the movie.

Every Christmas, my parents, my sisters, my brother and I used to watch the 1951 movie *Scrooge.* It is my most significant Christmas memory. Here, in my hour of need, came a character from that movie, visiting like some ghost of Christmas past. (Well, it was a ghost, and it was from my past...)

There in my mind was old Marley, wailing inconsolably, and dragging all those *chains* behind him. As I watched him in my mental movie, I realized that stress overload, for me, was like an endless series of chains, weighted down with endless responsibilities, with no rest in sight.

Like Marley, we wear the chains we forge ourselves. And just as he visited Scrooge to warn him to change his ways before it was too late, I had the idea that old Marley was visiting me. Here was the perfect way to warn the folks in my seminar about the effects of those chains of stress.

Now I knew exactly what I had to do. I left the office. I went to Wal-Mart.

I bought some bright yellow poster board and some black felt-tipped pens, and carried them back to the office. I spent the rest of the afternoon and evening making paper chains and signs (remember the ones we used to make in kindergarten?), each one for a specific stress that was weighing me down.

The chains were the easy part. Once I had that picture of Old Marley in my mind, the cause of my overload was very clear to me. All those responsibilities and *shoulds* were just the chains I had forged in my life.

I resolved right then and there to reduce the number of chains I was carrying and to help other people to reduce their chains, too.

Now that I had identified the "problem," I was confident that there had to be a solution. And, if I was going to be able to apply it to my own life, it would have to be simple. I didn't have the stamina for anything really complicated. If I was going to teach it, I would have to be able to live it.

I thought of all the things I'd learned about taking care of myself. It occurred to me that I had learned how to take care of myself on two levels in the ten years since I'd chosen to take on that responsibility. There was my physical self to care for, and there were also my mental and emotional requirements to consider.

I'd been taught that only a healthy body could meet the requirements for mental and emotional health, so I started with the physical portion of my solution.

In the 12-Step Meetings I had been attending for several years, I learned the concept of "H-A-L-T." The letters in the word *halt* each stand for a specific behavior. It's a reminder on two levels: first, the minute you notice that you feel uncomfortable or upset, stop whatever you're doing immediately. That word "halt!" has the same urgency as it would if it were spoken by the military police at what was once the Berlin Wall.

Second, pay attention to the way you feel and choose your behavior. If you're *Hungry, Angry, Lonely or Tired* take care of the immediate problem first. *Before you take any other action*, take care of your physical or emotional needs. If you're hungry, eat. If you're angry, feel your feelings and try to work them out for yourself or call your sponsor. If you're lonely, call someone who cares about you. If you're tired, sleep.

It may come as no surprise to you that during all those years in places where I simply did as I was told (or something just the opposite), I had never learned to take care of my own needs. When I learned the concept of H-A-L-T, it was the very first time I had ever received permission take care of *me* first. Learning the specific strategies for taking care of myself had changed my life. I had no doubt that these strategies were instrumental in helping me to manage myself in the midst of my current circumstances. They would have to be an integral part of my program.

The concept of H-A-L-T had provided me with my first two physical strategies, sleeping and eating. It seemed to me that there should be three or four, so I kept thinking about possible solutions. Then I remembered how I learned to develop the habit of jogging.

I lived in San Diego in the mid-seventies. One day I realized, that as a person in my twenties, I was too young to feel as tired and stiff as I did. I was doing manual labor on a submarine dry-dock, but I wasn't exercising at all. Shortly after this great realization, I read an article in a magazine about teaching yourself the skill of jogging in 30 days.

I copied the article, and I tried the procedure.

I remembered the sense of accomplishment I felt after that first 30 days. I'd never done anything like that in my life! Once I finished the first 30 days, I ran four to six times a week for the next three years. Then my knees began to warn me that I needed another alternative. I was still walking for about an hour three to five times a week, because it made me feel good. I still do, and it still does!

Now I had three of the pieces of the physical solution: sleeping, eating, and exercising. I had an idea for putting them together. Still, there was something missing.

As I continued to consider the possibilities of the final physical strategy, I found that I was using just the one that would work.

In order to keep myself focused on my project without getting too tense, I had unconsciously begun to breathe in the slow regular way that I had learned when I was living in San Diego. Until that moment, it never occurred to me to share that behavior with anyone.

While I lived in San Diego, I started practicing yoga. I learned a breathing exercise in *Richard Hittleman's 28 day Exercise Plan*. Even though my practice of yoga was (and still is) sporadic, I had continued to do this breathing exercise on a regular basis.

The reason for that was simple.

When I got stressed out, it seemed that my chest would just lock up. As a result, I could hardly breathe. Over the years I found that using this method of breathing during those times would relax me within minutes. Not only that, I discovered that this breathing seemed to have an overall calming and relaxing effect on me even when I wasn't stressed.

This breathing method would have to be one of the physical strategies for reducing the impact of stress.

Because it seemed so basic, I christened this breathing method *Breathing 101*. Later, when I was presenting this program in an all-day format, I added an advanced breathing technique, *Breathing 102*. This was simply a deeper, slower variation of Breathing 101. I used it when I was trying to get to sleep at night. I also found it very useful when I wanted to relax enough to sit quietly, without being bothered by racing thoughts or worries. You can find it in the Extra Toppings Section at the end of this book.

It's hard to remember how *basic* all of this was in the beginning. *Stress Arresters* has evolved so much over the last eight years; I've forgotten some of the early forms that it took. It's easy to remember the process of creating it, though. Once I got the picture, it was just a matter of making more pictures to finish out the program.

It was a lot like visualizing a pizza, and then getting the ingredients together.

Once I had the physical strategies for my program, it was time to consider what mental strategies would just as basic and useful.

The Four T's are the result. The name comes from the fact that the title of each strategy begins with the letter T: Talk Nice to Yourself, Take the Positive, Try Smiling, and Take Time for YOU Everyday. These four strategies seemed to me to be the common denominators of all the positive behaviors that I had learned over the years. Most of all, they were the four that I used most often. They were the ones that had proved to be the most beneficial in reducing the impact of my own stressful circumstances.

How can I remember all this? I never forgot it! The program was successful, and I had a lot of fun presenting it all over town. People who saw it would tell other people about it, and I got a lot more invitations to speak than I could ever have predicted. For over 2 years, I travelled around town with my box of chains.

Then something momentous happened.

In late November, 1989, a geologist named Chuck Beatty called my office to ask me to present this program to the people in his Production Department. He had been referred to me by an engineer in his company who had hired me several months before.

In the course of this first conversation, he told me that he thought I was just what "his people needed." I had no idea at the time that he was just what *I* needed, or that he would think that I was just what *he* needed!

Because of *Stress Arresters*, I met Chuck Beatty, the love of my life. Since January, 1990, he and I have been partners in all things. In March, 1990, we started our company (formerly MEA Productions) and I began the full-time speaking career that continues today.

Chuck's life has changed because of *Stress Arresters*, too. After two years of wholeheartedly supporting me as I lived my dream of speaking and training, he found himself at a crossroads. Laid off as a geologist in the downsizing of the oil company where he had worked for seven years, he had the opportunity to choose a second career.

It had been his secret dream to become a graphic artist, a dream that had been buried in the pursuit of a "secure" profession. With his security lost in the downsizing, he decided to take the risk of pursuing his dream. The results are yours to see.

It's Chuck's artistic genius that created the stress chains in the PBS *Stress Arresters* video. He created the video cover and the cover of this book. He designed the layout and the illustrations you'll find throughout the book. All the graphics you will see in any of our products are Chuck's great work.

Because of *Stress Arresters*, we have been given the opportunity of a lifetime to work together. Miracle of miracles, our dreams are complimentary!

It has been my privilege to share this program with thousands of people across the country over the last nine years. I have found it to be a most effective program for combatting the effects of stress. I say that from my own experience and from the comments I've received from people who have tried it. I use it every day. It is my sincerest hope that you will benefit as much from using it as I have from developing it.

Let's find out together!

Part One:

The Dough

Stress and Your Life

What is Stress?

According to my *Webster's Collegiate Thesaurus*, stress is simply "the action or effect of force exerted within or upon a thing." Other words that mean the same as *stress* are "pressure, strain [and] tension."

Seems pretty straightforward, doesn't it? Straightforward, and unemotional. When you listen to people who are experiencing stress, though, stress seems to be much more complicated. It's certainly *discussed* with more emotion.

Years ago, because I was experiencing a great amount of stress in my life, I decided to do a little investigating about it. Since I've always been a fan of Sherlock Holmes and usually have several dictionaries at my disposal, I became a sort of *stress sleuth*. In the process, I discovered some very interesting things.

First of all, I found out that there were three words that were used to describe this "action or effect of force exerted upon a thing." The words were *eustress, stress* and *distress*. Let's take them one at a time.

First, the word *eustress* . The "eu" comes from the same Greek root as the word *euphoria* and it means "good." *Eustress* describes the kind of "action or effect of force exerted" that's beneficial and invigorating. It's the kind of stress that's necessary to have, in order to actively participate in your own life. It's the kind of stress that propels you to greater achievement and success; it motivates you to strive and grow.

I never found this word in any of my dictionaries, though. I found it on the cover of a book. *Eustress* was the title of this book, which proposed, in detail, that a certain amount of stress is critical for a healthy and productive life. Although I've never found this word anywhere else, I'd certainly like to get it back in circulation.

Next, there's that word you hear all the time, *stress*. Just to see if I could discover a different angle on the word, I looked it up in my *Mosby's Medical Dictionary*. Here's the definition I found: "any emotional, physical, social, economic or other factor that requires a response or change." Once again, it seems pretty simple and ordinary.

Then there's the final word in our trio: *distress*. The "dis" comes from the same root as *disease* and it means "bad." In fact, the "dis" part of the word *distress* is a prefix that comes from the Latin word which means "apart, asunder." To be more precise, according to my *American Heritage Dictionary of the English Language*, the word *distress* means "1. Anxiety or mental suffering. 2a. Severe strain resulting from exhaustion or an accident. 2b. Acute physical discomfort. 3. The condition of being in need of immediate assistance."

Now we're talking! This is what people have been describing as *stress*. This was the word that described what I was experiencing when I started playing Sherlock Holmes.

This was a great revelation to me. At the time I just filed it, but the information comes in handy now that I want to set the stage for our discussion of stress. Because I believe that words are important to our understanding of anything, it's important to agree on our terms.

This book is about managing your response to stress, *in order to significantly decrease (or eliminate) your experience of* distress.

Stress, once again, is that "emotional, physical, social, economic or other factor that requires a response or change." When you think of stress in that way, it becomes possible to consider that it is, by nature, neither a positive nor a negative thing . Will Shakespeare might have said it best when he wrote, "There is nothing good or bad, but thinking makes it so."

Now that we've agreed on our definitions, we can begin to arrest our stress.

The first thing we'll do is discuss the origins of several common responses that people have to the stresses in their lives, so we can discover how they experience so much distress. Then we'll explore some practical alternatives.

Origins of the Stress Response

How do people get from the experience of responding to those "factors that require a response or change" to "the necessity of immediate assistance?"

Apparently, there is one critical element which sends some of us over the edge. What matters most in the experience of stress as positive or negative, say the researchers, is the *meaning* we give the factors to which we must respond.

Once we've identified those factors as negative, we have two choices, as far as our body is concerned. We can either put up a fight or flee the scene. Our nervous systems are hard wired that way, as were our ancestors' nervous systems when humans lived in caves. The good news is that this *hard wiring* is one of the reasons that the human race survived long enough to make it out of the caves.

The bad news is that once we've identified a particular set of circumstances as only negative, we've succeeded in limiting the survival options available to us. As we approach the 21st century, having only two choices of behavior is no longer enough to *keep up*, let alone get ahead. That's the difference between our lives and the lives of our ancestors.

For our cave dwelling forebears, life was much simpler. Maybe an animal would show up to steal some of their food. Maybe the members of another tribe would come into camp and try to drag off some of their women—the quick way to

19

start a new community. Maybe the camp would be invaded by a whole group of hostile humans, or a pack of hungry animals. No matter what the situation, those cave dwelling folks had two courses of action from which to choose: stand and fight, or grab your stuff and get the heck outta Dodge! This was not a big problem. It didn't take an Einstein to figure out what to do.

In the late 1990's and into the future, we will continue to be bombarded with much more information and many more choices. Our lives are speeding by at a much faster pace than any human has had to deal with in the history of humankind. In the last 20 years, the world has changed more rapidly than it did in all of the previous 500. In the last 5 years, the available information in the entire world has doubled—*twice.*

It's been reported that, by 1995, the rate of available information in the world doubled every 18 months. As I write this, the World Wide Web is touted as the place to be *now*, if you want to be in business in the next five years. *Two years ago*, only a handful of scientists and academics had any idea that the Web even existed!

By the year 2000, it's been suggested that the amount of information in the world will *double every 9 months!* It's enough to make your head spin just thinking about it.

There is so much going on all around us. "Fight or fly" falls so far short of the mark of what is required for survival, it's laughable.

First of all, who could you possibly beat up and hope to get away with it? Fighting doesn't work anymore, unless you want to do it professionally, and what kind of choice is that for those of us who don't have the stamina of George Foreman? Just think of all the resources we have for those folks who resort to violence to reduce their stress: jail, prison, the Phoenix Project for Batterers, etc.

"Fight" is not much of an option, so how about "fly?"

Ha! Do you know how much it costs to fly these days—airline prices have gone through the roof! Where would you fly to, anyway? The world has become a Global Village and the stresses of civilization will follow you wherever you go. There is no escape.

So even though we still have the instinct to "fight or fly" in response to threatening situations, we have different constraints than our ancestors did. We must respond in a civilized manner. So we clench our teeth, hold our breath, and try to keep our head up as we survey what seems to be a hostile environment, from behind the projects piled high on our desk, wearing the closest approximation of a smile that we can manage.

It's not a pretty sight.

Given this, why would anybody want to add more of a burden to life than the one which the Information Age already presents?

Strange as it may seem, many of us have added one more straw to this camel's back. It's the one belief that weighs just enough to break us.

Some people actually believe that their worth as a human being is directly proportional to what they can produce. Their sense of who they are is reflected back to them in only one kind of mirror: their job title, their income, what they do. Their only measures of their own value come from things like the car they drive, the house in which they live, the clothes they wear and the associations to which they belong.

Sacrificing little pieces of themselves along the way seems like a reasonable price to pay—until all those pieces start to pile up, and they realize what they've paid. And what they've lost.

That's when they get their names in the paper: the front page, if they're famous enough, or in the obituaries, for the rest of us.

I know it's hard to believe, but some of us take better care of our lawns, and our cars, than we do of ourselves.

We would never dream of taking our cars out on the road without regular maintenance checks or a set of tires that can still grip the road. Even so, there are decent, law abiding folks out there who seem to believe that as long as they look good to other people, they don't need to pay much attention to how they feel inside, much less how they look to themselves.

"The What-I-Do-Equals-Who-I-Am Syndrome" is an insidious little belief. It can start the negative cycle of self neglect which, once started, seems impossible to escape.

Fortunately, there is no such thing as impossible when it comes to *Pizza and the Art of Life Management*.

First of all, *you* don't have to worry. You're reading this book! Second of all, I have the antidote to that insidious little belief. Here it is:

The idea that what you do equals who you are is a LIE.

What you do is nothing more than what you DO.

Who you ARE is so much more than that.

Now that you have the antidote, you need never be concerned about that lie again. I have heard it said that humans were created in the image of their Maker and that "God don't make no junk!" There never has been, nor will there ever be, anyone in the Universe exactly like you. You're unique and irreplaceable.

You don't have to take my word for this, either. Check it out for yourself. All you have to do is ask someone who loves you this question: "What is it about me that is so unique?" Then listen to what they tell you.

Odds are high that this person will be able to show you a version of yourself that will amaze you. From the perspective of someone who loves you, you possess so many fine, and thoroughly amazing qualities. Who you are, when seen through their loving eyes, is a glorious creature full of light and love.

Think about it. Describe somebody YOU love, and you'll see what I mean.

Moving right along...

So. Where are we? We've discussed stress as being neither negative or positive, we've addressed the amount of change the world is currently undergoing, and we've addressed how crucial it is to understand that we are so much more than what we do.

Please understand the most critical element that we've discussed: That it is the feelings we have about any situation that determine how we respond to it.

If you're experiencing feelings of being overwhelmed and overwrought on a regular basis, it's very likely that you will experience one more negative side effect. When bombarded with this kind of emotion on a regular basis, your brain can become so clouded that you can hardly think.

This is a major liability in the Information Age.

You will find that the future belongs to the people who can *think*. This quality means more than education; it means that you must be able to use your mental faculties under adverse conditions. If the world around you is in chaos, you must possess the inner stability to get through it.

These days, your survival depends on your ability to think on your feet. Far from a fist fight or an escape plan, what you need is the personal resilience and the mental stamina to find your way to your goals despite the obstacles you encounter. In order to do that, you've got to understand what you're dealing with.

First, we'll investigate the stress response (what happens to you physically when you decide that you're in danger). Then we'll explore the circumstances under which you make that decision.

The Stress Response

The term "stress response" was coined by Dr. Hans Selye in the early part of this century.

Dr. Selye was born in Vienna, Austria in 1907. He earned his M.D. and Ph.D. at the German University in Prague, although he spent his professional life at the University of Montreal. His specialty was experimental medicine. His identification of what he called "the General Adaptation Syndrome" (what we call the "stress response") secured his place in medical history.

Dr. Selye discovered that the body responds in specific ways to stressful stimuli. It happens in three stages: Alarm, Resistance and Exhaustion.

Let's take it step by step…

For instance, you are approached by a stranger in an alley *or* your boss is doing your annual review today.

First, your brain sends you a warning. Selye called this the *alarm* stage. Hormones are se-  creted, as your body prepares to ward off an attack. This is the first indication that something is wrong. *No matter what is actually happening*, your body is preparing to fight off an attacker or run away.

Scientifically, here's what happens: there is an increased secretion of hormones which affect appetite, glucose (sugar) tolerance, susceptibility to infection and the ability to heal

25

wounds quickly, among other things.

The hypothalamus is stimulated, affecting body temperature, sleep and appetite.

The "fight or flight" response is activated when the adrenal medulla (part of the adrenal gland, located over your kidneys) secretes norepinephrine, a hormone that acts to increase blood pressure. All of this activity increases adrenaline flow. There is increased activity of the sympathetic nervous system (the system that controls the acceleration of the heart rate, the constriction of the blood vessels and the blood pressure).

If the problem is a minor one, you can handle things at this level. For instance, your review is a good one *or* you outrun the attacker, all the way to the police station. Once you've responded to whatever caused the alarm, all the affected systems in your body return to normal functioning. You are ready for the next alarm.

The human body has responded to danger in this way since humans lived in caves. If it's not one darn thing it's another—but the danger is usually over with soon enough. You can rest up for next time.

However, if the stressful situation is *not* short-lived, the body will adapt itself to responding on a long term basis. For instance, you live in a neighborhood where personal attacks and murder are daily occurrences *or* your company is in the process of reorganization and people in every department have been getting laid off, sporadically, for the last five years.

If this is the case, then your body will move past the Alarm Stage into the Resistance Stage. There's no big crisis here, just a continued physical defense. You just grit your teeth, put your shoulder to the wheel, and forge ahead. It's a lot like the storming of the Bastille—on a daily basis. Because you're physically and mentally on the defense, it's unlikely that you're getting much rest. Your entire being is focused on survival.

Scientifically, here's what happens: The hormone secretion returns to normal, and the "fight or flight response" disappears. All hormone levels return to normal. We adjust to the stressor; we just tolerate it.

Your body, if well cared for and strong, can take this kind of a beating occasionally with no ill effects. A week at a time, maybe even several months at a time, in rare circumstances. What's critical is that you are not experiencing this kind of beating in more than one important area of your life.

These days, though, it's not occasional—it's chronic. More often than not, this kind of stress is happening in several important areas of your life, because everything is so interconnected. A friend of mine describes this as the bone-grinding stage, where you just get worn down by the unrelenting circumstances in whichever negative situation you're involved. After awhile, you find that you can no longer think straight or move quickly, despite the consequences.

This bone-grinding overload is a dangerous situation to be in for long. An overload of stressors, or an increase past your personal tolerance level for long enough, without relief or rest, will result in the final, Exhaustion Stage.

For instance, a major gang war is taking place in your neighborhood, your spouse has just left you, your oldest

27

child has run away from home and the doctor's office called to say you need a biopsy *or* You've run out of departments to transfer to in the downsizing in your company, your spouse lost his job two months ago, the bank is threatening to foreclose on your mortgage and you get a traffic ticket for speeding home to check on your mother, who has just moved in with you and your family.

We've all been exhausted before, and survived it. We've all lived through the occasional major crisis. Sometimes it just happens.

The danger comes from chronic exhaustion, which can kill us by weakening our immune systems so we can no longer fight or fly on any level. This is the most dangerous stage for those of us who have adapted to unreasonable demands. When you don't pay attention to the overload, you're a sitting duck for a major accident or illness.

Scientifically, here's what happens: The hormones secreted during the Alarm Stage are now secreted at very high levels. That is, there is a great increase in the secretion of hormones that affect appetite, glucose (sugar) tolerance, susceptibility to infection and the ability to heal wounds quickly. Our heart rate increases, our blood vessels constrict and our blood pressure rises.

In the Exhaustion Stage, we lose our ability to respond to the alarms which are a natural response to increased demands. We have depleted all of our physical resources, and have no other defenses. The next stressful situation we face, no matter how small, will be too much for us to handle. It is likely to result in physical, mental or emotional collapse, and possibly death.

Let's put this in perspective.

In a recent magazine article, twenty-five percent of the people surveyed admitted that they felt that they were at the point of chronic exhaustion—all of the time.

Twenty-four percent of them reported that their fatigue has lasted more than two weeks.

It has been estimated that 5% of the population of this country suffers from "chronic fatigue syndrome." It will come as no surprise, then, to learn that fatigue is listed as one of the top five reasons that people visit their doctor.

There's one tiny piece of information I'd like to highlight here. *The stress response starts in the brain.*

Every one of the stress responses I've just described occurs on the basis of what we *think* is happening. Our thoughts determine our response.

In his book, *Rational Emotive Therapy, A New Guide to Rational Living*, Albert Ellis suggests that we don't perceive reality. He says that we respond to how we *feel* about what we *think* is happening, despite what actually occurs.

So all of this "fight or flight" stuff may not have anything to do with the situation we currently face! Unlike our ancestors, we can frighten ourselves over "nothing" on a regular basis.

How can this happen?

Your Brain and Stress

The impact of stress affects our bodies for a very good reason. This reason will become more obvious, though, once we investigate what happens in your brain. You'd be amazed at the things you can learn about stress when you start checking up on your brain.

For the purposes of our discussion, we'll consider three main sections of the brain. These sections are based more on function than on form. That is, we'll be more concerned with the kind of behavior that originates in each section, rather than their physical attributes or location.

To keep this as straightforward as possible, let's call these sections the Primal Brain, the Limbic System and the Modern Brain. These names are not the ones that you're likely to find in textbooks on brain function, although they're useful here. By the time you finish reading about them, it's likely that you will understand their functions so well that you'll recognize them in any medical textbook despite their scientific names.

What's important to our discussion here is that each one of these sections has specific attributes. Once you understand them, you will know exactly what section of your brain is commanding your behavior at any given time. Best of all, knowing about these brain sections can provide you with a gold mine of information about your responses to stress.

Let's start with the Primal Brain. This is the oldest part of your brain. The Primal Brain has three general functions: to find food, to locate predators, and to recognize and pursue mating partners. That's it.

When it comes to these particular activities, the Primal Brain is the section on which you want to depend. Each one of these behaviors is so finely tuned that they're practically instincts. You don't have to think, you just react to circumstances.

The next section of interest is the Limbic System—the Seat of Emotions. I imagine it as a roaring fire over which you can cook whatever you want. It adds fire and vitality to whatever you're cooking. It increases the energy of both positive and negative behaviors.

Last, and certainly not least, is the Modern Brain. You may have heard this referred to as the Cerebral Cortex. It is the part of the brain that makes us human, because it gives us the ability to *think*. No other animal has one, no matter how intelligent they are. (It's the part of your brain your parents were talking about when they said "Use your *brain*!!")

The cerebral cortex is the part of your brain that integrates the mental faculties of intelligence, abstract thought and choice-making. It's the part of the brain that oversees perception and behavior.

"Now *what* does all this have to do with stress," you may be thinking.

In fact, it has an astonishing amount to do with it.

Consider this: In order to actually put into practice all the strategies we'll be discussing in this book, you've got to be able to engage your Modern Brain.

When you are on overload, what we call "stressed," the only part of your brain that's working is your Primal Brain! *This* is the part of your brain that sends the "fight or fly" signal to your body. This is the part of your brain that's in charge when you *react,* instinctively. The Primal Brain is the most ancient part of your brain. It doesn't need much care or feeding to maintain its instinct to survive.

Sometimes this behavior is referred to as being on "automatic pilot." You do what you always do without much conscious thought, as if your behavior was on a computer program. (Have you ever found yourself in the driveway of your home without any recollection of how you got there?

31

It's the same phenomenon as a horse always finding the barn.) What little flexibility you have is focused on eating, keeping yourself out of trouble, and…well…you know, the mating partner thing.

Now, the Primal Brain is very good at the tasks for which it's responsible, but it's no match for the Modern Brain when it comes to dealing with the demands of the 21st century.

The Modern Brain is the part of your brain that must be operating in order for you to be able to consider the circumstances you're facing, and what you need to do. Only when this part of your brain is operating, are you capable of responding; using your Modern Brain is the only way you can *choose your behavior.* This is the part of your brain that keeps you one step ahead of the competition; it's the home of your creativity and resourcefulness. It's the part of your brain that gives you the resilience to cope with constant change and social chaos.

Unfortunately, in order to function at its highest capability, the Modern Brain must be cared for exceptionally well. It's just like an expensive violin, or a high performance racing car. If you don't take care of it, your extraordinary Modern Brain won't be able to do what you want it to do.

Once the Modern Brain shuts down for lack of the proper requirements for optimal operation, the Primal Brain is, once again, running the show.

A scary thought.

What kind of care does the Modern Brain require? It requires a well rested body to be strong enough to respond to the challenges of the 21st century. It requires enough energy to cope with the constant flow of information that must be dealt with immediately.

If you compare the energy requirements of the Modern Brain and the Primal Brain, you'll get a better idea of what I mean.

The Primal Brain operates on very little energy. Because it operates on the level of instinct, it doesn't need much information or energy from the rest of the body. It's basically pre-programmed to do the three things that it does. (Of course this is grossly simplified, but you get the idea.)

The Modern Brain, on the other hand, is a very technical apparatus. Just like a specialized mega-computer, it requires a certain level of power to perform its specialized tasks.

If you think about an IBM 286 computer or an early Macintosh (less than 10 years ago!), you may remember that the amount of computer power it took to run a program on either one of them was significantly less than it takes to run one today. Today's computers, of the same size or *smaller*, are so much more powerful, and so are the programs we use in them.

A program that requires the power of Pentium chip or a Macintosh Power PC would not even *start*, let alone do what you need it to do on one of those older computers. It's the same way with the Modern Brain: in order to make use of its superior capabilities, you must supply it with enough energy. Just like computer power requirements, the amount of energy you need has increased over the last five years. What used to be enough is no longer sufficient.

The Modern Brain requires a huge amount of physical energy to perform effectively. When you're physically exhausted, it's hard to do anything more complicated than react. You only have enough power to run your Primal Brain.

Using the strategies detailed in the Four Week Plan and the Four T's will help you to keep your Modern Brain in the best performing condition. You will have the strength and the stamina to choose your responses to life, despite any negative circumstances you may encounter.

You won't ever be at the mercy of your Primal Brain again—or anybody else's either!

The Bottom Line

We've discussed the fact that the stress response starts in your brain, and that there are specific physical responses to the message from the brain that you are "under attack."

It's the *meaning* that we give to circumstances that ignites the brain's response to send a message to the body to "fight or fly."

With this in mind, there is one more thing to consider. It's something that we often overlook. That is, once we adjust to increasingly demanding circumstances in one area of our lives, we need to reduce the demands in another area to "balance the load."

Trying to be superheroes in every area of our lives can pose the greatest challenge to our health and well-being. When we run out of steam, we're surprised to find out that we can't operate in high gear indefinitely.

Our bodies have been programmed for our survival. When we remain unaware of the processes we set in motion, we only hasten an overload on the system.

The Chains

Now that you've digested all this theory, let's have some fun. Let's take a personal look at one woman's experience of stress overload...

Those of you who have seen the *Stress Arresters* video will remember "the Chains." If you haven't seen the video, you can still get the idea by reading the following section.

Let me introduce you to Moira, the Trained Professional.

This is a woman with an important job, family responsibilities, social and professional obligations, and a habit of saying "yes" to everything.

The words that follow are her words. (If I know her, she'll just keep on going until she runs out of steam...)

"So you want to know about stress, do you? Well, I am an expert on the subject! It's *very* complicated, but I'm just the person to explain it to you.

"Now, you've already heard about that all that "fight or fly" stuff. Many people think that this is what really causes all the problems in our lives.

"I don't think so.

"Something else is really going on, and I just so happen to have a sample of one right here. It's this bag I carry around everywhere, my Bag of Stuff.

"Not only does it weigh a ton, this bag is full of all those things I can't possibly live without. These are important things. (My goodness, there are a lot of them! That's why I need to have a bag.)

"You might even have one yourself. If you do, there's a good chance that my bag has some things in common with yours.

"First of all, the bag never matches my outfit. Worst of all, it has this unfortunate tendency to fall open... right in front of the *last* person I want to see my stuff!

"It takes a huge amount of effort to keep a grip on that bulging bag of stuff, keep it closed, keep moving and manage our two choices of fight or fly!

"It's not a problem for me. I'm a trained professional.

"You are, too? Well, let me tell you what's in my bag, and we'll compare notes."

(As Moira pulls out her first piece of stuff, you think you hear the sound of chains rattling. The sound is coming from inside the bag...)

"The biggest part of my stress is my *job*.

"I am a *trained professional*.

"I've got to keep this grindstone right up close to my nose so I don't forget what I'm doing or get completely out of control!

"I have a million things to do every day, and I never know what my boss will dream up next.

"Why?

"Because this is the dawn of the 21st Century, and they keep changing all the rules around here on a daily basis.

"It's not a problem for me, though, because I know exactly what my REAL job is, anyway.

"My real job is to prove to everybody, everywhere, just how *good* I am.

"I do it. I do it well. And I look good doin' it, too!

"Of course, this is not a problem. As I've already told you, I'm a trained professional.

"Now if this was all the stress I had to handle, you must believe that I could do it with my eyes closed, standing on my head.

'Unfortunately, I have a bag, so you know there's more.

"The next part of my stress is my *spouse*.

"Believe it or not, there's a very good reason why this chain is a little bit smaller and a little bit cuter than the first one.

"That's because this one is *so fine*! He's about 6'3", he's got these big, beautiful eyes, and he's in touch with his feelings. (Just the way I like a man to be!)

"He's a great cook, he helps me around the house sometimes, and occasionally he will even get those clothes out of the washer and put them in the dryer...

...sometime between the time that they're done, and the time that they mildew.

"But, hey, he does what he can.

"Now this man has a really stressful job, too. He's a graphic artist.

"He spends all day long in a little bitty room...
...by himself...
...*coloring*.

"It's very stressful for him.

"So when he comes home from his long hard day… of coloring…he's really tired. That's when I start my other job.

"Now, I want you to know that when I come home from my long day at that stressful job, I have another job to do. That's right, I *am* the little woman.

"I've got my apron on, I've got my hair pulled back, and I'm wearing my bunny slippers.

"When that man gets home, I run to meet him at the front door. I have his slippers in one hand, and his newspaper in the other. I say, "Sweetheart, darling, baby! I've got dinner cooking and it's gonna be on the table in *five* minutes. You just pull up a chair and relax, honey. I'll take care of everything. *I'm* a trained professional!"

"Just like *you* do.

(Yeah, right!)

"When that man comes home—carrying those stupid crayons—I say, "Don't you start with me! I'm tired, I'm busy, I've had a looong day! I've got a real job—I'm a trained *professional*! No, I *don't* have dinner ready, we're havin' *fast food*!"

(Just like you do. Right?)

"Well, let me tell you something else! I found out that the men in this world aren't havin' any more fun than we women are.

"When they come home from a long hard day at the job, all they really want is a little re-spect, right?

"And what do you think they say they get?

"They say all they get is that long list of chores to do instead of a hot cooked meal and their slippers!

(Yeah, well.)

"But we all handle it, don't we? We handle it well. And we look good doing it, too.

"And I'll tell ya why we all handle this spouse business so well—it's because we know that there's a very good reason why God gave us spouses in the first place.

"It's so we wouldn't be *bored* after work!

"Yessirree! I'm on a roll now...

"Those of you who have *children*, know why I have *cats*!

"You knew there was a reason that you wanted to have these little darlings in the first place, right?

"They were going to be sweet, and smart, and cute. They were going to do everything you told them to do, the minute you told them to do it.

"They were going to bring pride and joy to your entire family!

"They were going to wear the clothes you bought for them, no matter where you bought them *at*...

"But Noooooo. It didn't work out like that, did it?

"There you are, sitting on the couch with your feet up on the coffee table. You got a cup of decaf, and you're just trying to RELAX for a few minutes, before the next CRISIS erupts.

"Next thing you know, your daughter walks in to your line of sight.

"This girl has got her hands on her hips, and she has got "The Walk."

"And she has got "The Sigh."
(Huuuunnnnnngggggggggghhhhhhhh! and the Eye Roll.)

"And this girl is wearing a black bra on the **outside** of her clothes.

"Now *this* takes the cake!

"You thought you'd seen everything, but this is beyond your wildest nightmares.

"Your jaw drops right to your chest. All you can do is stare.

"This girl pulls herself up to her full height and looks you in your face. She says, 'Mother. Father. I don't know what's the matter with *you*...

...Because *this* is the *real* me!'

"You cannot speak.

"The girl is *seven years old!*

"But you handle it.

"You handle it well.

"And you look good doin' it.

"Because you know that even if you can't *stand* it, she's your kid!

(Now that ought to be enough for anybody to handle at one time, don't you think?)

"Suuuure it is.

"However, I've got the industrial strength size bag—so I've got *more*.

"So. In addition to handling all the things I handle on a regular basis, I want you to know that there are a lot of times...

...when what I'm *thinking*...
and what I'm *saying*...
don't match.

"It's not a problem for me,
though, because nobody knows.

"And the reason that nobody
knows...

...is because nobody *cares*!

"They don't pay us what they
pay us to come in and tell them
how *we* feel. They pay us to come
in, do our work, do somebody else's
work, do 10% more just because
we can, do it all with a smile on
our face, keep our mouths shut,
then go home and come back in
the next day and start all over again.

"It's not a problem for me.

"I'm a trained professional.

"Now. Just when you think that ought to be
enough for any one person, I might as well admit to
you that there's more.

"For instance, in addition to *all* the things I do, for
all the people that I do them for, I do things for
people I don't even *know*.

"Like the other night, for instance. I was sitting in
my kitchen—it was about 11:30.

(You want to know why I was sitting in my
kitchen at 11:30 at night?)

"Well, you know that feeling that you get when
you have just dropped off to sleep? When you have
finally f

    a

      l

        l

          e

into that **chasm** of unconsciousness...

...and your brain kicks in, saying,

'You forgot to do this! You forgot to do that!'

(I *hate* when that happens.)

"So I decided that, *this night*, I would sit up and *wait...*

...for whatever it was, that I hadn't done, to *occur* to me.

"Because it always does...

"So there I was in my kitchen, waiting for the inevitable.

'Fifteen minutes later, the phone rang. (Now you know when the phone rings at quarter to midnight, it is *not* good news.)

"I picked up the phone right away and I said, 'Hello...'

"This woman on the other end of the line said, 'Moira?'

"'Um-hmm', I said.

"'This is Sister Mary Perpetua', she said, 'from Saint Patrick's School, and I really need your help. We're having a PTA meeting tomorrow morning at 7 a.m. (she paused) I've taken care of everything, but I've forgotten the refreshments!'

(Another pause, as I held my breath...)

"Then she said, 'Do you think you could bake 15 dozen cookies for me for tomorrow morning at 7 o'clock?'

"If there is any doubt in your mind about my answer, you've obviously missed the fact that *this* was my mission from God!

(Incidentally, I got my entire education in Catholic schools. If there's one thing I remember from Catholic school, it's that you *never* say *no* to a *nun*!)

"So you know what I said, don't you?

"I said, '*Of course*, Sister, don't you worry. I'll take care of all the cookie details. You get some rest... I'm a trained professional!'

"Now you might be wondering where I'm going to get all these cookies in the middle of the night.

"There's always somebody who suggests the all-night grocery. 'Hey, ma'am, they're open 24 hours!'

Nuns can *tell* the all night grocery.

(Your *dog* can tell the all night grocery. 'Hey, ma'am, you didn't bake these yourself. It doesn't count!')

"Now under these circumstances, you've got to have a secret weapon.

"And I've got just the one.

"I get it at the all-night grocery, in between the milk for the kids, and the beer.

"It's those cookie dough rolls—you know the ones I'm talking about. They make these industrial strength size cookie dough rolls, and you can make 10-12 dozen cookies out of each roll if you do it right. I've got 10 or 12 rolls in my freezer all the time.

(People want cookies? I GOT cookies!)

"Now the secret weapon part of all this is that when you're making cookies with this cookie dough roll, you can actually do two things at once.

"*If* you know what you're doing.

(You know how this works, don't you?)

"You get that cookie dough roll and you slice it up until it looks like you got a pile of hockey pucks. Then you cut those hockey pucks into quarters, like little pieces of pie, and you line them up on a cookie sheet. Then you mush 'em down with your finger and slide that cookie sheet into the oven at 350° for 10 to 14 minutes, depending on what kind of cookies you're making.

(Now I was making four different kinds of cookies, because that's just the kind of woman I am.)

"So the real secret to this kind of cookie making is that you can actually take a cat nap in between batches!

"So there I was, doing two things at once. Line up the cookies, stick 'em in the oven, set the timer, take a cat nap. Take one load out, line the next load up, stick 'em in, set the timer, take a cat nap. Pull 'em out, line 'em up, stick 'em in, set the timer, take a nap. Pull 'em out... stick 'em in... set that timer... take a naa....

(silence)

"Huh!

(Big sigh...) I don't know what time the timer went off.

"All I know is that I woke up, at 3 am, to the *smell*...of something *burning!*

And I couldn't remember how many cookies I had baked. Since I'd rather *over* do it than *under* do it, I made seven dozen *more* cookies.

By the time I finished, it was 5 o'clock in the morning.

I had to be at the school by 7—and you *know* how long it takes me to look this good—

Two hours! It's all special effects!

"So I got in the shower, got my hair and makeup done, coordinated my outfit, got all those cookies on a big silver tray with doilies under them, and rushed out the door! I sped through traffic, drove all the way across town, and I got there *four minutes early*.

"Those people thought I was a gift from Heaven.

(Alright. I was a little tired.)

"I was a little disoriented.

'But I KNEW that if I stepped off a curb and got hit by a bus, I would go *straight* to Heaven...

"Because I would have *died* in the service of my fellow human beings!

"I...was...fabulous.

"It was a great day for the PTA!

"And it was all because of *Me*. All because of me....

(snore) Zzzzzzzzzzz.

"Oh excuse me. I'm so sorry. I must've just dozed off for a moment. Maybe we ought to have this conversation another time...

"No? (Oh.)

"I'm sorry. You opened this book in the first place so you could meet me and learn all about handling stress, right? And if I think you're going to let me sit down on the job, I got another thing coming, huh?

"You're *absolutely right*.

"No, I don't want you to feel bad.

"And please don't worry about it—nobody *else* lets me get away with sitting down on the job, either.

"But you know what? Sometimes I just get so *tired*, all I want to do is *rest*. And *nobody* lets me get away with it.

"It's alright, though.

"Really. I don't want you to worry about me. I'm a trained professional.

"And I have another secret weapon!

"Oh, you want to know about it? I've got it right here in my bag.

"Every once in awhile, when I have had it up to *here* with doing everything for everybody all the time with no rest in sight, do you know what I do?

"I go down to my local saloon, and I have me a coupla beers.

"Now, there's something about a coupla beers that *reduces* my stress!

"Two beers takes the edge off my stress.

"Fourteen beers eradicates my stress!!

"Now, I live in Texas, where we have those long neck beers. (Of course, the more you drink of 'em, the longer the necks get!)

"And let me tell you, while I'm drinking my beer, I forget about all that stuff that stressed me out.

I forget who told me I wasn't doing it right, what papers I forgot to file, where I put "the numbers"...

...what my name is...where I parked my car...

"But I don't *care*!

"'Cause for a coupla hours—or a coupla weeks, depending on my vacation schedule—I am not stressed!

(Snort)

"But—oh—excuse me...

"It's probably not very polite to be waving this beer bottle around in your face. It's probably too early in the day to be drinking anyway. I'll just put this back.

"Sorry.

"Hey! Have you got a cigarette?

"No?

"Oh.

"So? What? You don't want me to smoke?

"Jeez!

"I know what it is, you're worried about me, right? You think I'm go-ing to catch some disgusting disease, don't you? Yeah, something really bad—like emphysema, huh?

"Now lemme ask you a question.

"Could you *spell* "emphysema" before you read it in this book? (I didn't think so.)

"Here's the deal: if you can't *spell* it, then you can't *get* it!

"Anyway, there's a *very good reason* why I smoke.

"If I didn't smoke, I would *eat,* and I got enough problems in my life without having to listen to a buncha jerks telling me I'm gettin fat!

(Oh yeah, right.)

"You think if I don't want to gain weight, I should exercise?!!

"What are you, crazy? I'm too *tired* to exercise! I couldn't exercise if my life depended on it!

"What's that?

"You think I don't take very good care of myself?

"Well, I got news for you. *I do too take care of my self!* I got the proof right here in my bag!

"Wait a minute, I'm getting it-it's right here...just a minute... "I got it!

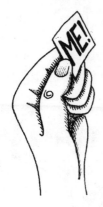

"I spend this much time on myself, every *six years* ! It's in my appointment book...

"Alright, so it's 3 o'clock in the morning when nobody else wants to see me—but it's IN there!

"You don't think I'm doing this right, do you? You think I'm taking care of everything for everybody else and I'm not doing a very good job of taking care of ME.

"Well, *I don't care what you think*!

"I've got a headache *this big*, and it's got this stupid conversation all over it!"

WAIT! Don't close the book!

I told you I'd be back, and I'm back. Really!

(Whew! When that Moira gets in a lather, she sure gets in a *lather!* I guess she makes her point, though...)

If you're thinking about your own stress chains, you're in the right place. Keep reading...

(Feel free to take a break, or get a glass of water, too.)

The Chains Workpages

Does what just happened seem familiar?

Based on the responses of thousands of people across the country over the last nine years, if Moira's baggage is familiar to you, you're in very good company!

Not only that, most of us get here with all the best intentions. In the midst of all the things we're trying to accomplish, we never take the time to think about how we got so overloaded in the first place.

Since you're reading this book, chances are good that you would like to discover how the things in your life got out of hand. Fortunately, discovering this is the first step in taking control of your life again.

Why not take a few moments to start the process right now?

Here's how you do it.

1. Get yourself a cup of your favorite refreshing beverage, and go someplace quiet, where you can think. (Leaving the house for a park or even a library is a good idea, too. What's important is that you find someplace where you can relax without being disturbed.)

2. Fill in the answers to the questions on the worksheet below. You can do this on a separate piece of paper, or right here in the book.

3. Take some time after you've completed filling in your answers to look over what you've written. You may find that there is a pattern to your stress. If you have any other thoughts about the pattern or the process, write those down, too. You can use this information as a starting point for your stress reduction program. You can also look back on it, sometime in the future, and see how far you've progressed!

Chains Worksheet

(Note: please adapt this worksheet to your own needs. Use the chains as a metaphor for your stress, or use a different one that you like better. Use all the blanks, use some of the blanks, or add extra ones if you want to. What's most important here is to diagram your stress—and you're in charge of the picture.)

My Biggest Stress Chain is:

Another big chain is:

Another big chain is:

Another big chain is:

Some of my other chains are:

Carrying all these chains feels like:

Much of the time I wish that I could:

Some of the people and things I have listed as chains are important to me. They include:

I am willing to learn how to handle the load more effectively in the future, so that the things I care about will no longer be burdens.

(Sign here) _____

Random thoughts, comments:

Patterns that I noticed:

Part Two:

The Sauce

The Physical
Strategies

The "Bite at a Time" Theory

The process of handling the elements of your stress "one bite at a time" is a simple one. You begin in one place (as I have with Week One of the Four Week Plan). Then you systematically continue through each element until you have addressed each one of the sources of your stress.

It's likely that you will see a pattern. Once you do, you can use what you've learned to deal with all subsequent stressful circumstances. You will have created a plan from which to work, and you can use this plan as a starting point or your blueprint for the future. It's up to you.

It works the same way with eating pizza. After you were introduced to eating pizza, you probably developed your own way of doing it. For instance, do you eat the crust first—or last? Do you pull off the toppings one by one, or do you chance burning the roof of your mouth by biting right into the hot mozzarella? When you think of pizza, chances are you know exactly how you're going to eat it. You may eat it the same way that you ate your first piece of pizza. On the other hand, you may have developed your own unique way of eating pizza, after conducting some field research.

(When I was a counselor, the term "field research" was used to describe what some people needed to do to decide for themselves whether what the counselor had suggested was true. Since I'm a big "field researcher" myself, I like to offer it as an option up front!)

You can use this book in your own unique way, too. You can learn to develop your own system for taking care of yourself, and you can depend on it. More than that, your system can serve as a personal diagnostic. You can check yourself against the Four Week Plan and the Four T's (for starters) to discover where you might be out of balance. You can make adjustments based on what you discover.

You can take the whole process to a higher level for yourself. It all begins with "one bite at a time"!

The Alternative...

Please understand that there is an alternative to "one bite at a time." I know about it because I've experienced it. It's what happens when you don't have a plan.

Without a plan, we are faced with two kinds of options on a regular basis. We can choose to take care of ourselves, or we put aside our own needs to take care of someone or something else.

Neither of these options is inherently positive or negative. Both of them are appropriate in certain situations. The problem arises when we choose only one option, all the time.

Most of the time, it doesn't involve taking care of ourselves.

Chances are, we are likely to volunteer to take on another job or responsibility until we become so burdened that we simply can't manage another thing. Not only that, it gets harder and harder to manage the stuff we were responsible for in the first place.

Seems kind of crazy, doesn't it?

We don't do it because we're crazy. We do it because we're very responsible people. Unfortunately, many of us believe one of the most insidious lies of the modern age.

The lie is that "what we do is who we are."

Some of us seem to feel that if we don't do a whole lot of things for a whole lot of people all the time, that we won't have any value. If we don't feel valuable in the first place, then this is an easy trap in which to fall. This is the trap that gets us when we're not working, not helping, not employed, not in the middle of things, not hearing from other people that we're needed.

Once again, it's not what's happening, it's the meaning

we give to it. I once knew a woman who was so invested in the business of *doing,* that she was on the phone to her office on the morning that she was having brain surgery!

How does this happen?

It happens because we do what we are taught to do by people with the best intentions.

How many of us were raised to take care of ourselves *first* by our loving and well meaning parents? More likely we were taught to do the things that would help us to get along better with others, even at a cost to ourselves. Of course, our parents were trying to do their best by us, helping us to be good and polite citizens.

The bottom line is that so many of us were rewarded for putting our needs last, because that was the responsible thing to do.

So it's likely that most of us continued to behave in ways that were rewarded. That's not surprising, because this is how all children (and animals, for that matter) learn.

Oddly enough, neither one of these alternatives is inherently destructive. Either choice could be the best one in any situation. It's the *ability to choose* that is the critical element here. Because giving a choice to a child who is learning *takes longer*, many people have not been given this option.

So, true to our training, we work and work and work. We try to get approval and recognition from other people for choosing their requests over our needs. We all need to feel good.

Unfortunately, that's not the usual result of this behavior.

More likely, the result is a vicious cycle. We can never seem to get enough of what we need. Few people will sit you down and suggest to you that what you really need for peace of mind comes from the inside. Why would they, when you're doing such a great job of taking care of them?

Two Important Points

When I was embroiled in this vicious cycle in my own life, I learned two things. I mention them here because I believe that developing this program was a direct result of recognizing and understanding them.

Point #1: The idea that "what you do is who you are" is a *lie*.

I don't know who started it, I only know that it doesn't work. I've met a lot of people who have hurt themselves for a long time, trying to prove its truth. I haven't met anyone who's succeeded, although I have no doubt that a lot of people have died trying.

There is an antidote to the lie. It is the belief that *each one of is a Miracle, just because we exist.*

It has been said that each one of us on the planet is as unique as our fingerprints. There never has been, nor will there ever be, a person exactly like you on this earth.

That's an awesome compliment, as well as an awesome responsibility, if you think about it.

One of the first things we can do to be able to handle that responsibility is to "lighten up" on ourselves. If each one of us is a Miracle, just because we exist, then we weren't put on this earth to be ground into a powder!

Point #2: I finally realized that nobody was going to drop out of the sky to take care of my stress, or anything else in my life. That's when I knew I had to give up my Superhero fantasy. I had to find a realistic way to handle my stress.

It was harder than I thought to give up that Superhero fantasy, though. I guess I watched too much Mighty Mouse when I was a kid.

Have you had those fantasies, too? You know, the one that goes like this:

Enter, Stage Right: Huge Superhero, muscles flexed, with a warm & tender smile, just for you.

Superhero: " Ta-Da! I'm here to take care of your life! You got a *problem*, I'll *fix* it. You got a *worry*, I'll *handle* it! You need anything at all, you just let me know. I'll take care of everything!"

You: "Oh, I thought you'd never get here! I'm so glad you've come! Just pull up a chair. I've got a big pot of coffee brewed for us. It's going to be a loooonng conversation!"

Fade to a brilliant sunset...

Wouldn't it be great to have some great big, powerful super-being show up to take care of all those pesky problems?

It hasn't happened yet!

Which brings us back to the "one bite at a time" theory of stress management.

That's where the Four Week Plan comes in.

Once you've identified some of the causes of your stress, you're ready for the next step. You are ready to start the plan that can help you to reduce the effects of stress by helping you to increase your physical stamina.

The Four Week Plan works like this: once you understand that you are in complete control of your life, you can deal with your stressors one by one, systematically. You can accomplish this by choosing to change one small habit a week, for four successive weeks. These changes will provide the groundwork for the stress management program that you can build on for the rest of your life.

No matter what else you may have read about quick fixes for stress, it will take you every bit of the four weeks to develop your new habits. The overload didn't accumulate overnight; you'll need more than overnight to deal with it.

Our old habits have been with us for years. Even though these habits provide us with shortcuts to decision making in our daily lives, the price we pay for them is having our brain on automatic pilot. In order to make new decisions, we have to develop new habits. We have to consciously choose to make the necessary changes. It takes some work and effort, and it can be done.

By choice and repetition, we can develop those habits that will greatly reduce the impact of stress on our bodies. The payoff for the work it takes to do this is that we feel better physically and we're less likely to overreact to anyone or anything.

A Few Words About Affirmations

If the process of practicing the physical strategies was a sandwich, understanding the concept of "one bite at a time" would be the bottom piece of bread. The Four Week Plan would be the top piece of bread and Affirmations would be the meat in the middle.

Understanding and practice, alone, are not enough to keep the process working over time. The state of mind that you bring to the process is the critical element. That's where affirmations come in. In any great sandwich, it's the stuff in the middle that makes all the difference. You'll find the same thing is true when you begin practicing the Physical Strategies with affirmations.

This section is about the process of affirmations: what they are, how they work, how I discovered them, and what their purpose is in this book.

What are Affirmations?

If you look up the word affirmation in your favorite dictionary, you'll probably find a definition like this one: "Something declared to be true, a positive statement or judgement."

The root word, "affirm" means "to declare positively or firmly, to declare to be true." Another word from that root is "affirmative", and it means "positive, optimistic."

(When people say "yes, that's true" in the military, they say "that's affirmative.")

An affirmation, as I use the term in this book, is a positive statement of what you believe to be true, *even if you have not experienced it yet*. What's important here is that you are willing to consider it. It's your *willingness to believe* what you say that makes all the difference in your experience.

Great minds over the centuries have suggested that you will get what you *think* you will get, whether it's useful to you or not. It is my belief and my experience that this is true.

Have you ever heard of people who are described as being able to "snatch victory from the jaws of defeat?" I'd bet you a dollar to a doughnut that their beliefs are very different from those of people who are known to "snatch defeat from the jaws of victory!"!

For the moment, I would ask you to consider the possibility that your beliefs structure your reality.

Put another way, what you believe is possible has everything to do with what you actually experience. As an illustration, have you heard the story about the four-minute mile?

There was a time, over forty years ago, when no one had succeeded in running a mile in less than four minutes. There was a sense in the track and field community that it just was not physically possible for a man to run that fast for that long. Despite what *everybody* knew to be true, in 1954, a man named Roger Bannister succeeded in doing just that.

What secret weapon did Roger Bannister possess that no one before him had? Even though I can't prove this, it's easy for me to believe that he had an affirmation about his ability to do something that no one else had ever done before. More than that, he had to have believed it before he experienced it. That took some mental strategy.

Once he had proved it was possible, anyone else could do what he did. As a matter of fact, one month after Roger Bannister's feat, another man ran a mile in less than four minutes. The next year, thirty seven people ran the mile in less than four minutes. In the following year, three hundred runners broke that record!

If it's been done, you can do it. If it hasn't been done, you can still do it. The only thing you need is the willingness to believe that you can.

How Affirmations Work

There are three specific components involved in the process of affirmations. First, we have to go back to the brain.

There is a "functional" system in the brain called the Reticular Activating System. By describing it as functional, as opposed to physical, scientists admit that they know what it does, not *where it is* exactly.

It's the same thing as knowing that a cat has the ability to purr. Although the mechanism for purring appears to be somewhere in the throat of the cat, that mechanism has not been identified physically. There's no "purr box." In the same way, the Reticular Activating System is not located in a specific place. You couldn't point to it in the brain, *and* it still functions as a specific system.

The Reticular Activating System (RAS) acts as a filter. If all the sensory information that was available to you on a daily basis got through to your brain, you would go insane in a couple of minutes from sheer sensory overload. So the RAS filters through only the information that you've decided that you need.

For instance, have you ever purchased a new car? Before your purchase, you may not have noticed how many cars of that particular make or color were on the road—it wasn't in your filter. However, after your purchase, you are amazed to find all the cars of that make and model and color driving right alongside you! The information is now in your RAS.

Affirmations act as requests to your RAS to set up filters for the kind of experiences which you desire. That's the first part of the process.

We are constantly giving ourselves affirmations of one sort or another. Other people are constantly giving us affirmations of one sort or another, too.

There are also *denymations*, negative statements of what could happen. ("Denymations" is not a real word. I just made it up to differentiate between the positive affirmations and those statements which deny that anything positive can happen.) Denymations work just as effectively on your RAS as affirmations do.

Apparently, your brain doesn't differentiate between positive and negative. It doesn't differentiate between what we call "reality" and what we call "imaginary." And all thoughts create physical responses.

That's the second part of the process.

All thoughts create physical responses?

Check it out for yourself. Imagine the face of someone you dearly love and pay attention to your physical response. Do you find that, as far as your body is concerned, you feel as though this person could be right next to you?

Now think about a chore that you really don't like to do. What happened? As far as your body is concerned, you might just as well be right in the middle of doing it—or trying to avoid doing it!

You've just demonstrated to yourself that your body responds to your thoughts. That can work for you or work against you, depending on what you're thinking!

So far we've discussed that affirmations work because of the Reticular Activating System, the filter in our brain, and that all thoughts create physical responses.

The third part of the process is the fact that repetition is critical.

If you hear something once, you may or may not believe it, especially if it's something you've never heard before. In fact, if you have any opinions which conflict with the statement, you may even discount it and forget about it.

If you hear something over seven times, even if you disagree with it, you have to pay attention to it. For some reason, *seven* is a magic number as far as our brains are concerned.

For example, commercials are just affirmations of what some sponsor wants you to believe. Run a few through your head and check it out. More importantly, once they've been repeated enough times, commercials can even be stored in your long term memory. You can probably still sing the entire jingles of commercials you heard ten or twenty years ago, although you haven't heard them in nearly that long.

(Which one is playing in your head right now?)

There's nothing wrong with commercials—some of them are even true. What's important to our discussion is knowing that because of constant repetition, the messages from commercials get past your RAS right into your brain. These messages affect the way you do things: what you buy, where you eat, what kind of car you drive. Once you have heard something seven times, you begin to notice it. If you hear it seven times an hour, eight hours a day, seven days a week over seven months, it becomes part of your life. No wonder they show commercials every six or seven minutes!

Affirmations—or denymations—that you have heard as often as you hear commercials can affect your life in the very same way. What you think you can or cannot do is the result of the information that has gotten through to your RAS, to which you have a physical response and that you can repeat from memory no matter how long it's been since you last heard it.

We're talking about a very powerful series of events.

This particular series of events affects us all of the time whether we are aware of it or not. I suggest that we can experience some spectacular results if we just pay attention.

The practice of using affirmations has been extremely helpful to me and that's why I recommend it to you.

How I Discovered Affirmations

My first conscious experience with affirmations came in 1986, when I read the book *Daily Affirmations*, written by Rokelle Lerner.

I had been involved in a 12-Step Program for the previous five years. I was practicing what I had been taught about how to "act as if." That is, if you think you don't know how to do something, find someone who does it, and do what they do. Act as if you know what you are doing, and pretty soon you really will. I've since heard that described as *modeling* the behavior of someone who is doing something you want to do. (and *that's* another book!)

At that time, despite the fact that I had learned how to copy other people's behavior, I was still full of negative self-talk. I would behave in a positive manner, then give myself a hard time about not doing it perfectly. Or I'd doubt myself and my own potential for recovery. It was like taking one step forward and two steps back.

Somebody told me about Rokelle's book and I bought it. There were 365 daily affirmations in it, one for every day. These affirmations seemed to address every possible recovery issue I was facing. Each page had a beginning affirmation, then a paragraph containing things to think about and a concluding affirmation. Frankly, reading it set my brain on fire.

It was the beginning of the "inside" work that I had to start. It turned out to be the perfect compliment to the "outside" (behavioral) work that I had been doing for the previous five years.

Despite the fact that it was slow going, the process filled me with hope. I read Rokelle's book every day, and soon found others like it. At one point, I had four books of daily affirmations by different authors. (I like to have options!)

By December of 1988, I had changed so much, on the inside as well as the outside, that I was in the process of making a new life for myself. You might have read about it in my first book, *Bootstrap Words—Pull Yourself UP!*

One day in a bookstore, where I was looking for a book that would help me to get through some challenging circumstances, I met two women. They were best friends, and they were chatting amiably with one another. They were standing right in front of the section in which I was searching. In the course of the conversation we had, one of them offered me the last copy of Louise Hay's book, *You Can Heal Your Life.* I've wished, ever since, that I could have found that woman again to thank her.

This is one aptly named book!

In Louise Hay's book I found an affirmation that described an "infinite well of Love" as being "deep at the center" of my self. It described each one of us as a beloved child, and it detailed specifically all the loving things I could do for myself to continue to heal. If you've read the book, you know the affirmation. If you haven't read it, I recommend it highly.

I made a copy of this affirmation and taped it to my refrigerator door. I said it out loud every morning and every evening for over a year. I even said it out loud in the middle of the day if I felt like it. I'm still amazed at the transforming power of those words.

When I was digging through all my files to write this

book, I found that piece of paper that had once been taped to my refrigerator door. So many of the things that I had affirmed aloud for myself are true for me today. Knowing this is one thing, but going back and actually seeing the evidence was astounding!

I still use affirmations every day. Recently, I found a book that was as significant to my understanding of the power of affirmations today as those first two books were to me back then.

In her new book, *Money Freedom: Finding Your Inner Source of Wealth*, Patricia Remele suggests that *the way* you say affirmations can affect how useful they will be for you. That had never occurred to me before. Now that I know about it, I want to make sure that you do, too.

This technique comes from a science called Neurolinguistic Programming (NLP), pioneered in the 1970's by John Grinder and Richard Bandler. It's called the "Belief Technique" and is based on the theory that you store information that you *believe* in a different part of your brain than you store the things that you *doubt*. To discover where you are storing your beliefs and your doubts, pay attention to where you move your eyes.

For instance, say something that you know to be true, like your name and address. "My name is _____ and I live at _____." Where did you move your eyes? (It's likely that you moved them up, because 60% of the population does. However, that means that you have a 40% chance of looking somewhere else!) The direction you move your eyes is not as important as *paying attention to the direction*. This is where you store your beliefs.

Now say something you know to be patently false. "My name is Pinocchio and I have green hair." Where did you look that time? Did you look down? Many people do—although not everyone. Once again, what's important here is to pay attention to where you looked. Did you get a feeling that time, that something wasn't right? Many people do. This is where you store your doubts.

Feel free to conduct some field research on this subject. Practice with several statements. Use things that are definitely true for you and grossly untrue for the best results. The more you test it, the more aware you will be of how it works for you.

Now what does this have to do with affirmations?

Just this: if you say an affirmation that you *don't* believe *and look in the direction of doubt*, you'll be reinforcing your doubt in what you're saying. We've already agreed that you get what you think you're going to get, right?

If you say an Affirmation that you *want* to believe *and look in the direction of belief*, your brain will very quickly store that message with your beliefs. You'll find that your affirmations will be much more effective in a much shorter amount of time.

Every time you choose to look in your direction of belief when you say your affirmations, you will reinforce your belief in what you're saying, *even if you have never experienced it*. You'll be amazed at your results. I've been using this technique since I read about it, and I wholeheartedly recommend it!

Now that you understand the process, I invite you to check it out for yourself.

The Purpose of Affirmations in this Book

Every strategy presented in this book comes with several affirmations to try. There is also space for you to create your own, now that you know how to do it.

You may find, as many people do, that beginning this simple program causes you some discomfort. If I've learned anything from the last nine years of presenting this program, it's that the discomfort is a surefire signal that you're moving in the right direction for yourself.

The discomfort is a signal that you are growing past your previous boundaries. You're stretching yourself! Just like the "growing pains" we experienced as kids growing from childhood to adolescence, the discomfort is a normal part of the process.

Using affirmations on a regular basis is very useful in working through this discomfort. It's like having extra help as you move forward, as you grow.

When I think of this process in my own life, I have a very clear picture of how it works. In my mind, there's a movie of a small child tentatively taking its first steps. If you've ever watched a little one learning to walk, then you know what I mean.

As the child maneuvers across and around the furniture, the parent is right there with a hand held out to steady the little one on her way. Before the child walks on her own, she has already practiced taking the steps while holding on to the hand of some loving grown-up.

In this process of learning to manage yourself in spite of circumstances, you might, at first, feel like that baby. The affirmations you will find at the end of each strategy can serve as the hand held out to help.

At this point, you've discovered the process of "one bite at a time" and the power of affirmations. You're ready to try the Four Week Plan.

The Four Week Plan

The Four Week Plan invites you to change one behavior each week, for four weeks. The goal is to reduce the impact of stress on your body by increasing your physical stamina.

The process is progressive. For instance, in Week One, you'll start one new behavior. In Week Two, you'll continue with your behavior from Week One and add the new behavior from Week Two. In Week Three, you'll continue with your new behaviors from Weeks One and Two, and add the new behavior from Week Three, and so on.

Using the workpages will allow you to track your progress over the next month. Be sure to repeat the affirmations you've chosen. When you follow the process, you'll be amazed at your results.

Week Number One: Picking a Bedtime

Have you ever found yourself wishing you could just lie down for one minute? That you could just lay the burdens of your life down for just a short while and sleep like your kids do? Sometimes we manage it: sitting in front of the TV in the recliner, or napping with your head down on the paperwork on your desk and the office door locked in the middle of the afternoon. "Napoleon and Churchill took naps," we tell ourselves.

Rest, not to mention relaxation, is the most vital part of any stress reduction program. Nothing else will work without it. None of us would consider driving our cars from Maine to California on one tank of gas, yet we think nothing of working from dawn to dusk with no rest and no breaks. (We'll talk about food in the next chapter.) We are *trained professionals!*

Week Number One is the week you can decide to get more *sleep*. Yes, it is that simple. Even so, it's not always easy. Most of us find it challenging to sit still for 30 seconds or more while we're still conscious.

There's always somebody, somewhere, who needs us to do some very important job that will make all the difference in our professional or personal life. We wouldn't want to be caught *sitting down on the job*, would we? Sleep just isn't something that most of us put in our schedules.

Think about it. What time do you get to bed? Adults all over America have been telling me for years that they get to bed: "Whenever I'm *done*."

What does that mean? That means 11:30 at night, 2:30 in the morning, 4:30 in the morning—or 5:00 in the afternoon after you drag your tired body into the front door and fall down, face first in the rug, snoring, until somebody comes in and says, "Hey! I need something!" Then you get up and say "Of course I can help you—I'm a trained professional!"

This translates to the ancient axiom: "No rest for the weary."

Now, what happens when you finally drag your tired, aching body into your bed? When you get there, do you go to sleep?

Survey says: "Of course not!"

And why does this happen? It's because your body and your brain have been fighting each other all day. Your brain's been screaming about all your responsibilities and your body's been whimpering about all the aches and pains you've been ignoring because you were so busy taking care of everything.

Your brain wins out during the day. But, when it finally screams at you to *go to sleep!*, your body has other plans...

So you're not getting to bed at a decent hour, and when you finally do get there, your body is too worked up to let you sleep. And you look this good! Imagine if you were getting some rest.

Would you be interested in a simple solution?

How about this: Pick a bedtime.

Every night for one week, get in bed at the same time—and stay there. Don't get me wrong. I don't presume to tell you what *time* to go to bed. That's your decision. You know how much sleep you need at night. It doesn't matter what time you pick, as long as you're consistent.

There are those people who don't like the idea of having a bedtime. They say that bedtimes are for children. Well, maybe so. But, what do the kids look like first thing in the morning? Wild and full energy, right? And what do you look like? Don't answer, it's none of my business. *And*, you get my point. We all need a bedtime.

The biggest challenge many of us face is remaining still for the first 30 seconds—or the first 30 minutes. Our brains kick in to remind us of all those things we forgot to do, or still have to do, or *might* have to do, to be ready for tomorrow.

Let me ask you a question here:

What happened to your "off" switch? Even a car or a computer has an "off" position. It's no wonder you're exhausted!

Picking a bedtime is a simple solution—and the challenge it contains may require all of your strength.

Some people might find it difficult to stay still on those first few nights. May I suggest that you're up to the challenge? If you will simply use all your willpower (and some of the relaxation exercises you'll find in this book) to *stay put*, you'll find that it will become a lot easier.

By the way, if you share your bed with another person, you may want to give them some warning before starting Week One. If they find you laying in the bed, for no good reason, at a time much earlier than normal, they may get ideas. You don't want to have to fend them off, or hurt their feelings. Why not use this as an opportunity to make an appointment for some private time together—before bedtime?

If you will consistently get in bed at the same time every night, you'll notice a big difference by the third or fourth night. By the end of the week, once your head hits the pillow, you'll be *out like a light.* You'll be amazed at the way you'll feel in the morning!

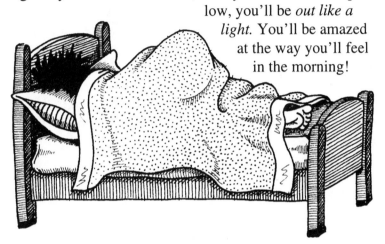

What you're doing is conditioning your brain and your body—your biological clock, if you will. By going to bed at the same time every night, your body and brain begin to *expect* to go to bed at a given time. It becomes easier to fall asleep.

People are sometimes concerned about the possible side effects of this new behavior.

Over the years, I've found that once you start this process and get really good at it, you do have to be careful. One of the worst things that could happen involves "planned deviant behavior." By that, I mean that you might want to stay up past your bedtime…

Consider a scenario that goes something like this: You've got a drink in one hand and a plate of hors d'oeuvres in the other hand. You're chatting away merrily, until your brain gives your body the signal you've programmed into it.

Your brain says, "Bedtime!" And your body says, "Sure!"

Your drink flies one way and your plate flies the other way, as you fall asleep on the spot with a smile on your face.

Yes, you've spilled that stuff all over the rug.

However, you're such a pleasure to be around these days, that your friends and family clean up the mess, put a blanket over you and never say a word! Nobody wants you to go back to the way you were before.

You'll have more stamina, you'll be refreshed in the morning, you'll start to get more done, and you'll be ready to start on Week Two.

For Those of You with Infants...

Do you have an infant living in your home? (An infant who is 6 months old or younger?)

If you have an infant who doesn't yet sleep through the night, Week One can pose a particular challenge. You don't have the luxury of a bedtime, no matter how desperately you may want one.

Your sleep is being interrupted at all hours of the night, because a helpless human being is depending on you for their survival.

Please recognize that you still need to get all the sleep that you can. Naps, as you can take them, are imperative for your health and well-being.

If you have a new baby, and other children who are small, *and still* believe that you should be doing everything else you used to handle so efficiently before your children came along, you will soon be of no use to anyone.

If you are working full time and have an infant who still wakes up during the night, *please* reduce as many activities as you can. Get as much sleep as you possibly can. Nothing else will be as beneficial to you as getting adequate sleep now.

You're going to need your strength when this baby becomes a teenager!

One great thing about kids is that they grow up. If you will take care of yourself now, you can do two valuable things for your family—you will be a calmer parent, and you will be teaching your children the invaluable lesson of self-care.

Whether we like it or not, we teach our children with our actions much more powerfully than we do with our words. You can choose to make your influence a positive one.

Affirmations For Week One:

✳ *I am willing to commit to resting.*

✳ *I deserve to get enough sleep at night.*

✳ *I listen to my body, and when I'm tired, I rest.*

✳ *I take good care of myself by making sure I get the rest I need.*

Write your own affirmations below:

Workpage: Week One—Picking a Bedtime

My Goal: *I will pick a bedtime and be in bed at the same time every night this week.*

Track your progress by checking off the days you meet your goal. Use the space provided to answer the daily questions that follow. (Please feel free to copy this information for your personal use, and make extra sheets as necessary.)

My bedtime is: _____

Daily Questions:

	Agree				Disagree
• It was easy to wake up today.	1	2	3	4	5
• I felt rested today.	1	2	3	4	5
• It was easy to get to sleep last night.	1	2	3	4	5

☐ Day 1

☐ Day 2

☐ Day 3

☐ Day 4

☐ Day 5

☐ Day 6

☐ Day 7

Week Number Two—Eating Breakfast

Congratulations on completing Week One. You did a
great job! Now you are well rested enough to deal with
Week Two.

This is the week we think about eating better. Even
though you may agree that this sounds like a great idea, this
week can pose quite a challenge for some of us.

When I mention "eating better" in my seminars, I've actually heard audible groans. For some people, talking about
healthy eating habits is like adding insult to an already upsetting situation.

From our friends, from our family, in books and magazine articles and TV shows, we're constantly bombarded by
conflicting rules about diet and nutrition. There's always
somebody who's trying to tell you what you should eat,
what you shouldn't eat, in what part of your anatomy all
those calories are piling up and what artificial sweeteners
are doing to mice!

There are more foods and "foodstuffs" on the market
now than there have ever been in the history of the world.
More people than ever before are struggling with their
weight, going on diets, eating on the run and feeling guilty
about what they eat.

We seem to have lost the tradition of learning about
food and nutrition in the home, in the tribe, in the community. Consequently, many of us are eating alone, at our
desks and grabbing whatever we can.

Most adults in America don't make a practice of discussing their eating habits with anyone. When I ask people
what they eat, they say, "Whatever I can, whenever I can!
Who wants to know?"

I have this theory that we all have our own four food
groups.

Mine used to be pepperoni pizza, crispy french fries,

root beer and orange sherbert. Whenever I felt that hungry feeling in my stomach, I would reach for one of my four groups. After inhaling as much as possible, as efficiently as possible, I knew I would have the strength to get back to work!

To add to our food problems, many of us also skip breakfast. We don't have time to sit down to something first thing in the morning. People in my seminars all over the country just close their eyes and groan when I mention the word breakfast.

You, too, may be familiar with a scenario that goes something like this:

It's morning, and you're late. You've gotten everyone else out the door on time, and now you have to scramble. You grab a big cup of coffee as you turn off the pot and race out the door.

You've got that coffee in a 48 oz. coffee mug with the name and logo of your company on the side of it. It's got a lid on it, so you can grab your coffee and rush out the door without spilling a drop on your business clothes.

You maneuver your way through rush hour traffic, listening to the radio to steer clear of wrecks, and polishing off those 48 ounces of java. That's breakfast in America.

Once you get to work, it takes a couple of hours to get your brain working at full throttle. It's at this point that the trouble begins.

At approximately 10:30 in the morning, something insidious happens in every office building in the country. The smell of freshly baked pastries is seeping in through the concrete walls and wafting down the hallways.

That smell is headed right for your face. When it hits, no matter what you are doing, you sit up straight and pay attention. That mesmerizing aroma has wafted right up your nostrils, and is headed straight to the pleasure center of your brain!

Before you know it, your nose has taken on a life of its own. You are now the victim of "Hungry Nostrils"—and if you're not careful, your entire body will be held prisoner to their demands!

You've got two courses of action, depending on your personal resources at the moment.

On the one hand, you could hold your nose and scream, "Get those things out of here, I'm on a diet!"

One the other hand, you could find yourself stalking the bakery cart to a secluded corridor, so you can reach out and grab *four* of those sugary delights.

Worse yet, you may find yourself stuffing those pastries into the pockets of your business suit, and sneaking off to find some privacy in the bowels of the building.

Once you're alone, you stuff all four of those things into your face at once!

"Aaaaahhhhhhhhhhh!!"

Once you finish your feast, you're sure to wipe the sugar off your face. It's not professional to walk around the office with sugar on your face.

No matter which course of action you choose, when lunch time rolls around, you're *starving*. Because your blood sugar has either skyrocketed and plummeted from that quick sugar high, or it hasn't had enough nourishment to get off the ground. Lunchtime, as everybody knows, is just another euphemism for "Pizza—Food of Champions!"

So you and your friends go to your favorite pizza parlor—where you eat seven pieces of Super Supremo.

Unfortunately, you don't even taste the first five. You're sucking them down with that powerful vacuum action. The last two you eat a bit slower—picking at the toppings and waving the crust around as you make a point to your colleagues.

After lunch, you're feeling very full, *and very guilty*. So you say to yourself, "That's it! I ate all that pizza and I've been trying to go on a diet, and I'm tired of feeling this way, and I'm not going to eat another thing for the rest of the day!"

When you finish your day at work, you go home and you cook dinner. It's the best dinner you've made in a long time. Your whole family is amazed. People you've never seen before are eating in your kitchen! (If you live alone, you cook for the whole block.)

This is one scrumptious meal—and not a drop of gravy or a speck of food passes your lips.

Your family and friends say, "Hey! This is great! Why aren't you having any?"

You say, "It's OK, I'm not hungry..."

"...No, I'm not sick, I think it's just post-nasal drip. You go ahead, you have mine."

After you've cleaned up the kitchen, put away all the dishes, attended to all those things that need your attention, it's close to 10:30 at night. And where are you?

In the kitchen.

You're in your favorite bathrobe—you know, the one with the big pockets. You've got your bunny slippers on. You're carefully making a list of all the things you need to re-member to take care of the following day.

Suddenly, you realize that the tractor beam from the refrigerator has got you by the seat of your robe, and is dragging you—*against your will*—straight to the refrigerator...

...where the little creature who lives in there is awake.

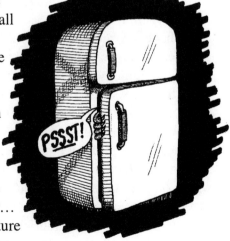

"Pssst!," it says. "You hungry?"

You gather up the last of your willpower and say, "I'm *not* hungry! I had all that pizza today and all those dough-nuts and I said I wouldn't eat anything else."

"Sshhh," says the creature. "You don't have to eat a lot."

"Yeah?," you say, eyebrows raised.

"Suuurrrre," it says, in a comforting voice. "You could just have a *little*..."

"A little?", you say.

"*Yeeaaaahhhhh,*" it says.

"Okay!," you say.

At this point, after checking to make sure that no one else is up, you eat a little bit...*of everything in there!*

Can we agree that this is no way to live?

No wonder you don't want to think about breakfast. Everything you eat that late at night is still sitting in your stomach, in the exact same shape it was in when it landed.

No wonder you're starving by 10:30 in the morning and suffering over baked goods.

And yes, there is a solution to this situation, now that you're rested enough to deal with it.

Your strategy for Week Number Two is to have break-fast every morning for one week. (Yes, I realize that you don't have any more time now than you did last week.)

There is, however, a new invention that can help you out with your strategy this week. It's those instant powdered breakfast drinks that you can pick up at your favorite gro-cery or health food store. There's a flavor to suit most everybody's taste, and it takes about 30 seconds to prepare.

And you've still got that 48-ounce coffee cup. Your strategy in Week Two could be as easy as simply changing what you put in that cup as you race out the door.

Of course you can still have your coffee—before and af-ter you have something nourishing to help you get through your day. Best of all, you will gain an added bonus.

When the baked goods come around during Week Two, and thereafter, your nostrils will be doing their normal job of holding up your glasses and making your face look cute—and you'll be busy working. You won't have to consider choosing between pastries or starvation. When the bakery cart comes through, you'll have the advantage. You will no longer have "Hungry Nostrils!"

Nobody says you can't have pizza for lunch, either. But this time, when you go to the pizza joint, you'll won't be starving. You won't vacuum down 7 pieces. You'll enjoy the 2 pieces that you do have—because that's all you used to *taste* anyway.

When you get home for dinner, you'll cook a regular meal and you'll eat it with your family and friends. Afterwards you'll clean up the kitchen.

At 10:30 at night, at the end of the first day of Week Two, where do you think you'll be?

In the kitchen!

Even if you're thinking you'll be headed for bed, I want to remind you that this is real life, not miracles.

You will very likely find yourself exactly where you always are at this time of night. However, because of the changes you made today, things will be a little bit different.

When that tractor beam from the 'fridge gets you by the seat of your robe (as it always does) and pulls you (against your will) to the 'fridge, you'll hear the little creature (who's not changing his life) whisper:

"*Pssst!* You hungry?"

Instead of reacting, you'll check!

Are you hungry? Nope, you've had three square meals today. You've been getting in bed at the same time for a week, and you're ready to go to bed.

Because you're working the Four Week Plan, you'll have the strength of will to close that refrigerator door. You'll turn out the kitchen light, and take yourself to bed.

If you will try this for a week, you'll really begin to notice a difference in the way you feel by week's end. Best of all, that little refrigerator creature will have to find a new place to live!

Affirmations For Week Two:

✳ *I am willing to commit to eating better.*

✳ *I deserve to give myself proper nourishment.*

✳ *I start my day with a nourishing breakfast.*

✳ *I take good care of myself by getting enough rest and having breakfast every day.*

Write your own affirmations below:

Workpage: Week Two—Eating Breakfast

My Goal: *I will eat breakfast every day this week.*

Track your progress by checking off the days you meet your goal. Use the space provided to answer the daily questions that follow. (Please feel free to copy this information for your personal use, and make extra sheets as necessary.)

Daily Questions:

I felt _____ today.

My energy level today was :

Making breakfast was (easy, challenging, etc.) today.

Other comments:

☐ Day 1

☐ Day 2

☐ Day 3

☐ Day 4

☐ Day 5

☐ Day 6

☐ Day 7

Week Number Three—Sauntering

Congratulations! You've been at it for two weeks!
You're getting enough rest at night and you're eating better. Now you're ready for Week Number Three. This is the week we start thinking about *exercise*.

You might be tempted to close the book right here. That's OK, you're not alone.

Most people I've spoken to will go along with the Four Week Plan to this point—right up until I mention the word "exercise." Given the horror stories I've heard, it's obvious to me that there is a very good reason for their hesitation.

Have you ever been taunted into exercising?

Have you ever reached the point where one too many people has made one too many comments about the size, shape, or flexibility of your personal physique?

The worst part of this torture is that it's always presented in terms of how you'd benefit from doing something you have absolutely no intention of trying, let alone doing on a regular basis.

After awhile, the verbal abuse gets to be too much.

"OK! OK! I'll *exercise!*"

And just when you think you'll get some relief by getting your well-intentioned family and friends *off your back*, you realize that this exercise thing is bigger than you had ever imagined.

First of all, it's going to cost you a lot of money.

You find out that all exercising involves special equipment. If you don't have the right equipment, you can't even start exercising. Without the right equipment, you'll be the laughingstock of your fellow exercisers.

So you cash in your stocks and bonds, raid your children's college fund, and take out a second mortgage on your house. Then you head down to the special exercise equipment store, with your wallet in one hand and your resolve in the other.

By the way, just in case you didn't know it, there is only one way for a *real woman* to exercise.

Aerobics.

And there is only one way for a *real man* to exercise.

Racquetball.

Armed with large amounts of cash and this critical information, you head down to your favorite athletic gear store. The men go one way; the women go another.

The men head to the *tough, macho, get 'em, beat 'em* athletic gear store.

You purchase your special racquetball shoes, especially equipped for all surfaces. You get your special racquetball socks that say *No Fear!* on one side and *Just Do It!* on the other. You get your special racquetball shorts: not too tight, not too loose. Just perfect—so that everyone will know that you are a *real* athlete.

Maybe you buy a racquet, guaranteed to take care of all the competition. Maybe you get a wristband and a headband, depending how you're feeling that day.

The women head for a completely different kind of store. It is the lovely, fabulous, accessorized and color-coordinated athletic gear store. This is the store that has video monitors strategically placed at eye level, featuring slim, trim, muscular and happy women in their perfectly fitting outfits, enjoying a workout that Jane Fonda would think twice about trying.

Undaunted by the sight, you buy those special aerobics shoes, and those special color-coordinated leotards and tights. You get a headband and a wristband, and that perfect shade of new lipstick to fully coordinate your fully coordinated outfit.

And every one of us, women and men alike, will purchase that one, last, *critical* piece of athletic gear.

We all get that oversized T-shirt to wear over the top of everything…so nobody will see just what it is we're working on.

Then we'll head down to that special place to commence our exercise program.

The men go to a glass-lined pit, lined with grandstands above—just like the Roman coliseum. Waiting inside, you find a giant, testosterone-filled behemoth, shifting his weight from foot to foot in anticipation of his next victim.

"Come on in, buddy," says the friendly behemoth. "You're next."

Undaunted, you think to yourself, "I've got my racquet, I've got my shoes, I can handle *this* guy!"

Fourteen seconds later, one little rubber ball has turned into thousands of projectiles that are zooming past your head at incredible speeds!

You try, desperately, to use every bit of skill that you possess. Unfortunately, it's not too long before your T-shirt is up over your head, your belly's hanging out, your socks are at your ankles, you have a terrible pain in your chest—and if you don't get out of here fast, you're going to have a heart attack and *die!*

Hero that you are, you face your opponent bravely.

"Excuse me, sir. I just remembered that I have an appointment right now *for a root canal.* Why don't we reschedule?"

And then, you *get out of there!*

Meanwhile, the women headed for the aerobics class

find that it is held in a room the size of a football field.

The room is lined with wall-to-wall mirrors. It is filled with these perfectly coiffured, perfectly made up, totally coordinated and accessorized women, who are not perspiring in the least.

They are not breathing hard.

They are smiling.

They are moving across the room—in unison, like a flock of birds.

And, they know what the heck that woman at the front of the room is talking about!

Undaunted, and armed with only your outfit and your determination, you jump into the middle of the action.

"I've got my leotards, I've got my shoes. If *they* can do it, then *I* can do it!"

That's when the fun begins.

As the group moves forward, you move backward. They move up, you move down. They move right, you move left. And what the heck is a "grapevine," anyway?

It doesn't take long for you to realize that something is terribly wrong here. "No problem," you think. Minor setbacks won't stop *you*.

You decide to stand in one spot, and *hop*.

For the rest of the class.

In an short time, your makeup is sliding off your face, your hair has become a wet mop, you have a stitch in your side, your chest hurts, and you know that if you don't get

out of there *right now,* you're going to fall down and
they're going to step on you.

So you *get out of there!*

And every one of us, women and men alike, say, "I said
I would exercise, and I exercised! And I will never, *ever,*
do that to my body again...

...and now I'm starving to death—I gotta have *pizza.*"

So it's perfectly understandable that the mere mention of
the word "exercise" is enough to give you the
shakes. Unfortunately, there is good news and
bad news.

The bad news is that you've got to
move your body on a regular
basis, or you will turn into
sludge at your desk.

"Yup, that was
Harry. He used to
work here. One
day, he just didn't
get up, so we had
him shellacked.
We have our cof-
fee breaks in
there with him..."

The good news is that I have invented an exercise that is
so easy that almost anybody can do it. (You still have those
shoes you bought the last time you tried to exercise, don't
you?)

Now that we've gotten the preliminaries out of the way,
let me tell you about my exercise. It's called "Sauntering."

All you have to do is stroll at a leisurely pace. Just move
your arms and legs. (If you move your mouth, you'll burn
up a whole lot more calories!)

In Week Three, after you've gotten two weeks worth of rest and a week of having breakfast, you'll be in perfect shape to start sauntering. You only have to do it for five minutes a day this week: two and a half minutes out, and two and a half minutes back. What could be easier?

Of course, some people don't think this is real exercise. They don't think that they will be breathing hard. Let me assure you, it's quite possible that some of those people will be *breathing hard.*

You might not have several hours a day to get to the gym or make arrangements to take that class you're already dreading. But, you certainly have five minutes a day to spare.

The secret to your success with this is to start with something simple that you know that you can do. Then simply continue with it.

That's much more effective than starting in the middle of something complicated and feeling like a failure because it's too difficult. If you think about it, I doubt you've ever heard about anyone who has succeeded at anything by starting in the middle. Each one of us has to start at the beginning, and build from there.

You've probably heard the comment that if human babies were as easily discouraged as human adults can be, we'd still be crawling around on all fours!

The difference between babies and some adults is that babies appear to consider themselves indestructible. No matter how many times they fall down, they get right back up. They start at the beginning, no matter how many times it takes to get it right. And when they do, look out world!

The same process works with exercise.

Surprisingly enough, if you give this a chance, you may find that you're enjoying this five minutes so much that you want to increase it to ten minutes the following week. You might even find that sauntering feels so good that you want to make some other arrangements in your life so you can continue to increase your "exercise time" in reasonable increments that suit you.

No matter what, you can set your own standards and limits. Best of all, you can follow your own progress. You may find that you no longer consider trying to meet up to the requirements of other people, for exercise or anything else.

Affirmations For Week Three:

* *I am willing to commit to sauntering.*

* *I deserve to feel good, so I give my body the exercise it needs.*

* *I welcome the energy that exercising provides my body.*

* *I take good care of myself by getting enough rest, having breakfast every day and giving my body the exercise it needs.*

Write your own affirmations below:

Workpage Week Three—Sauntering

My Goal: *I will begin my exercise program this week by sauntering for five minutes, five days out of seven.*

Track your progress by checking off the days you met your goal. Use the space provided to answer the daily questions that follow. (Please feel free to copy this information for your personal use, and make extra sheets as necessary.)

Daily Questions:

My energy level today was...
Scheduling my sauntering time today was...
Insights, Challenges, Victories, Important Notes:

☐ Day 1

☐ Day 2

☐ Day 3

☐ Day 4

☐ Day 5

☐ Day 6

☐ Day 7

Comments:

Week Number Four—Breathing

There is no doubt in my mind that you have done a spectacular job of the Four Week Plan up to this point.

By now, you've got a regular bedtime. You eat a good breakfast every morning and you've started an exercise program. What else is there?

How about *breathing*?

You probably think that you're breathing right now. Well, why don't you see for yourself.

(Go ahead, check. I'll wait.)

Did you notice any movement in your chest and shoulders?

Most people find that there isn't much, most of the time. There's a very good reason for this.

Many of us have been trained to keep our breathing to ourselves. (You wouldn't want someone to catch you in the middle of a bodily function, now would you?)

Because breathing is a semi-voluntary bodily function, you don't have to pay attention to it all the time. Whether you are conscious of your breathing or not, your lungs will take direction from your brain. Unfortunately, if the brain is sending "fight or fly" instructions, your breathing is going to be very shallow.

Shallow breathing is a great support to Primal Brain functions like running or fighting, but it doesn't do you much good if you need to *think!*

Your body will accommodate whatever kind of breathing you choose to do. If your face, shoulders and fists are clenched, your whole body will be tight. If your neck, back, stomach, rear end and toes are tight, your breathing can only be shallow. If, on the other hand, you consciously choose to override your brain's "fight or fly" instructions by breathing deeply and slowly, your body will respond by relaxing.

That brings me to our strategy for this week, *Breathing 101*. This strategy operates on the principle that it is physically impossible to stay tense if you are breathing slowly and deeply. Breathing 101 is the antidote to the stress response.

Breathing 101 involves two steps. (Important note: Please read the directions first before you try it. I don't want anything to happen to you when you're reading this book!))

Step One: you breathe air in through your nose, slowly and deeply. Pretend you are inhaling the delicious aroma of your favorite food—as if you could drink the smell. You pull the air down into your belly. Your shoulders and chest will rise.

Step Two: when you've inhaled as deeply as you can, you breathe out slowly through your mouth. Make a circle of your lips, and pretend you are blowing a sailboat across an imaginary lake. You 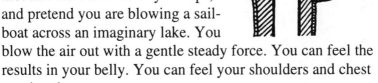 blow the air out with a gentle steady force. You can feel the results in your belly. You can feel your shoulders and chest moving down.

That's all it takes.

(No, it's not time for you to do it yet. Keep reading, because you may need to "warm up" to it.)

Some people have been breathing so shallowly for so long that it's very difficult to bring all that air down into their lungs and bellies. They get the air to their collarbone, and then they have to breathe out.

If you are one of those people, rest assured that you are not alone. In fact, the reason I know about it so well is because that's the way I breathed for years!

I have a trick that helped me. It has helped thousands of people across the country to be able to practice Breathing 101.

Remember those two steps I just mentioned? All you need to do is reverse them.

If it seems a little weird, let me explain. The reason that you can't pull fresh air any further down than your collarbones is because you are full of "1949 Air." (Don't get excited, this is not a year, it's a brand name.)

In case you're wondering, "1949 Air" is what each of us brings to earth with us when we are born. It's our job as humans to exchange that "1949 Air" with the air of the time in which we live.

Unfortunately, this has not been explained to most people. (Aren't you glad you're reading this book?)

Believe it or not, many people have been breathing so shallowly for so long, that they are walking around with the air that they were born with!

Even if you've never completely gotten rid of your own "1949 Air," you can start to do it now.

Before you start, read all the directions, and imagine what it will be like when you actually do each step. That way, you can give yourself a mental "dry run" before you actually do it.

To get yourself ready, it's best to sit comfortably in your chair. (If you are standing, place your feet hip-width apart, at about a thirty degree angle, so that you're balanced. If you're lying down, especially if you are using this to help you to relax enough to fall asleep in Week One, start out on your back for this breathing. You'll know when to move into your normal sleeping position.)

Gently get your body and your lungs ready for Breathing 101.

Take a few practice breaths—first *in* (softly, slowly and as shallowly as you need to) then *out* (as softly and slowly as you can) then *in* (see if you can breathe in just a *little* more deeply than the first time).

Now start your practice of Breathing 101 by breathing *out* as slowly as you can, for as long as you can. No matter how long or how short a breath you manage, when you've gotten out as much of that "1949 Air" as you can, slowly breathe *in* as slowly and as deeply as you can.

Do it again. Breathe *out* slowly and deeply. Breathe in slowly and deeply. Now do it again, and imagine that as you breathe out, you are blowing a sailboat across a lake. As you breathe in, imagine the aroma of your favorite food. Bring that smell into your lungs as deeply as you can.

OK—now that *you've read all the instructions*, why don't you take your lungs for a test drive?

Get in a comfortable position, close your eyes, and practice what you've read. *Remember to do this* S-L-O-W-L-Y. That way, you won't have to experience the unpleasantness of hyperventilating.

It's alright—nobody's looking.

Go ahead.

Really—I'll wait.

Wow! How was that experience? How do you feel now that you've tried it? A lot better, huh? Well you sure do it well. I bet if anyone had been looking, they'd have to admit that you look good doin' it, too!

Now that you know what you're doing, you can practice this as many times as you want to. You'll notice that after awhile (maybe today, or soon) that you can blow that sailboat across Lake Michigan, and that the aroma of your favorite food (or anything you choose) will fill every inch of your lungs and belly.

Now that you are aware of how it works, check your breathing regularly, every day this week. If you find that your breathing is shallow, stop what you are doing and practice Breathing 101. After awhile, you won't have to stop what you're doing when you need to practice Breathing 101- you will find yourself spontaneously breathing in the way that you have practiced.

The more you practice this, the easier it gets. You'll begin to notice how much better it feels to be breathing deeply. More than that, you may be amazed at how much capacity for breathing you have!

Just in case you have the same little voice in your head as I did when I began learning to breathe—you know, the one that says "this is so stupid!"—feel free to agree with it.

"Yep, this sure is stupid—and it feels *soooo* good!" When you don't try to fight your natural feeling of discomfort as you try some new behavior, you may find that you've worked through it.

Practiced enough, Breathing 101 actually becomes comfortable. There will come a day when your old way of breathing will be uncomfortable. Please feel free to allow yourself to take all the time you need to get there.

Please understand that I'm not suggesting that you attempt to breathe this way all the time. You'd look pretty foolish walking around in slow motion, taking deep breaths in and out with every step!

I am suggesting, though, that you take every opportunity to check your breathing when you notice that you are feeling tense. Many people have told me that they only recognize that they're feeling tense when they realize that they've stopped breathing!

After they've learned my breathing technique, they blow that deep "out" breath and take a deep "in" breath when they notice that their chest isn't rising. They've all reported a decrease in tension by simply concentrating on their breathing.

These reports of decrease in tension have their roots in your physiology. By concentrating on your breathing, you give your body time to relax enough to get the blood and oxygen to your brain and extremities. During the "stress response," blood goes to our stomachs to protect our insides from injury. To keep us from losing too much blood from our limbs in an injury, the stress response includes a decrease in blood flow to our extremities. (No wonder our hands and feet get so cold!)

When you practice Breathing 101, you are overriding your Primal Brain's "fight or flight" messages. You can't stay tense, ready to run or attack, when you are breathing slowly and deeply—it's physically impossible.

It's true that we can't always stop our natural reactions to stressful circumstances, whether they're positive or negative. We can retrain ourselves, though, to recognize the tension we're feeling and respond to it with this breathing technique. Try it at the dentist the next time you need a filling and you'll understand what I mean.

Finally, and perhaps most importantly, Breathing 101 opens the communication from the body to the brain.

Think about it—when your brain is shouting commands to your body, creating the "fight or flight" response, there is no two-way communication. It's like a general shouting orders to the troops. Can you imagine some sergeant coming up to the commander to tell him the men are just a little cranky today and would really rather lie down for a few hours instead of marching into some silly battle? Not bloody likely!

The same is true for your body and your brain. Your brain is like the general—and your body is like the troops. Your body does exactly what your brain says, until there's nothing left with which to fight. We call this exhaustion.

Your brain gives the order to relax when you use the Breathing 101 technique. It's like giving the body a holiday. All the troops are on leave, to respond in whatever way is appropriate to their energy level at the time.

So if you find yourself feeling inexplicably *tired* when you first practice this breathing, please lie down. If you feel hungry, go ahead and have something to eat. If you feel stiff or fidgety, please move around until you feel better.

Every time you listen to your body, you strengthen the communication between your body and your brain. You'll immediately reap two benefits: (1) you're less likely to go into a fight or flight response and (2) you're more likely to recover quickly if you have to fight or fly.

An Added Bonus and a Secret Weapon

Now that you have learned Breathing 101, you can use it any time. You can also use it as an alternative to the variety of things advertisers are constantly suggesting you to use to make your life better.

So, instead of relaxing by picking up a cigarette, having "one for the road," or ingesting pharaceuticals (legal or otherwise), remember to breathe. Instead of making yourself feel better by reaching for another fudge brownie, or charging something you can't afford on your new gold card, or sleeping with someone you don't *even like*, remember to breathe!

You now have a choice. Those other options will relax you in the short term, but the long-range consequences are probably more stressful than anything that's happening in your life right now.

Finally, Breathing 101 is a powerful social tool. If you don't believe me...check this out:

We all have those people in our lives who believe that the only way we're going to *get* what they're saying is if they get up our face and *scream*. You know the type, and you cringe inside whenever they come into your office. There they are, yap, yap, yap—so close they're fogging your glasses.

Want to know how to get rid of them? Sure you do.

OK, now that you know about Breathing 101, you have a alternative to holding your breath until you pass out. When you see that person marching in your direction, you *load up*. You take in a big hit of air as they approach. When they're a foot away, you let them have it (of course you did have pepperoni pizza with extra garlic for lunch).

"**H**i! **H**ow are you? **H**ow can I **h**elp you?" (You have to really lay it heavy on the H's, exhaling the whole way, for the best effect.)

I guarantee, they will think twice before getting up your face again!

Affirmations For Week Four:

* *I am willing to commit to relaxing.*

* *I deserve to breathe deeply and freely, so I practice Breathing 101 on a regular basis.*

* *I listen to my body, I know when to breathe deeply and slowly in order to relax.*

* *I take good care of myself by getting enough rest, having breakfast every day, giving my body the exercise it needs, and practicing Breathing 101.*

Write your own affirmations below:

Workpage: Week Four—Breathing

My Goal: *I practice Breathing 101 on a regular basis as I pay attention to my breathing at intervals throughout the day.*

Track your progress by checking off the days you met your goal. Use the space provided to answer the daily questions that follow. (Please feel free to copy this information for your personal use, and make extra sheets as necessary.)

Record your observations:

- How often I checked to see if I was breathing today:
- How easy it was to breathe deeply and slowly today:
- How often I noticed that I was tense today:
- The most remarkable thing I noticed about my breathing today was:

☐ Day 1

☐ Day 2

☐ Day 3

☐ Day 4

☐ Day 5

☐ Day 6

☐ Day 7

Part Three:

The Cheese

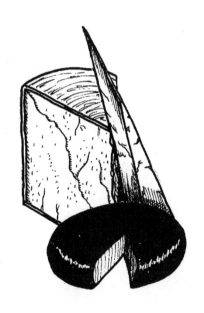

The Mental
Strategies

The Four T's

Once you've completed the Four Week Plan, your Modern Brain will be in much better shape. You'll know how to get past the Primal Brain's "fight or flight" response. Once you've done that, you're ready to take the next step.

When you start with the physical strategies, you change one thing a week for four weeks, adding each new strategy to the previous ones you have mastered. By the end of the four weeks, you will have made four complete changes.

The Four T's are a little different. They are the mental and emotional strategies that can help you stay in your Modern Brain. The Four T's are: Talk Nice to Yourself, Take the Positive, Try Smiling, and Take Time for *You* Everyday.

You can use them in any order. It's likely that mastering them will take more than a week, although some of them may be easier for you than others. With practice, however, the Four T's can become second nature to you.

Try these strategies one at a time. You can experiment. Discover which of them works best for you in any given situation. Try them until they become familiar, until it feels right to do them. You may find that practicing any one of the Four T's will make you more likely to try them again. Once you get comfortable choosing these behaviors, you will be amazed at the difference in your stress level.

I can't explain why this works, I just know that it does. It's not just that it works for me, either. Over the years, people who have attended my workshops have reported similar results.

The Four T's work like any positive process.

For instance, exercising makes it easier to do any other physical activity, right? In the same way, doing something to increase your positive response in one situation will make it easier to respond positively in another situation.

When you choose to use any of the Four T's, you're flexing your positivity muscles. Like concentric circles in a pond after a stone has been thrown in, the benefits can be felt in many areas of your life.

The closest I've ever come to an explanation for this process was something I heard at one of my first 12-Step meetings. I was in the Navy, stationed on a ship in Norfolk, Virginia. It was suggested to me that if I wanted to discover whether or not I qualified for the Program, I should attend 90 meetings in 90 days and check how I felt during the process.

At an evening meeting, the speaker was discussing the Promises of the 12-Step Program in detail. He was describing the potential for completely turning your life around, *if* the steps were followed exactly. Each step was to be concentrated on, in order, one by one, until it was mastered. Then you could proceed to the next step.

It didn't matter how long each step took to master, what mattered was that you stuck with the process. If you did, then you would begin to see the promised changes manifested in your life.

At the time, I was amazed that something so simple could be so powerful.

I remember hearing this speaker say that one of the promises of the 12-Step Program was that everyone who practiced it wholeheartedly would experience significant changes. The promise went something like this: "Things that seemed impossible to handle before practicing the 12-Steps would be handled easily, almost effortlessly."

I took them up on their promise. I worked the 12 Steps faithfully, even though doing so took great effort in the beginning. What I have found over the years is that I have incorporated those 12 Steps completely into my life. It requires very little effort to accomplish them now. The "new behaviors" I was learning then have become second nature to me now.

Like the 12 Steps, the Four T's have become second nature to me now. Yes, they were difficult to accomplish at first. However, the more I tried them, the easier it got.

When I was developing *Stress Arresters*, I had to distill everything I had learned about managing my own stress from a mental and emotional perspective. These four strategies are the result. Not only are they useful every day, they can provide an excellent diagnostic for those days when you're not feeling as positive as you would like.

Try them at your own pace. Experiment. You may be amazed at your results.

And for the record, you may want to document your progress.

Use this book, or create a separate journal for yourself. Once you've been practicing these strategies for awhile, you may want to read back over what you've written about your experiences. You might even discover that the journey has been more amazing than you imagined!

Affirmations For the Four T's

In each of the following sections, the affirmations are listed in ascending order. That is, each succeeding affirmation contains a more positive and active intent than the previous one.

Start with the affirmation that feels most comfortable to you. If all you can manage to do initially is affirm that you're willing to consider the possibility of using the strategy, then start with the first affirmation. Say it as many times as you need to, until you're ready to move down the list. If the final affirmation is comfortable enough for you to say, then start there.

Wherever you start, pay attention to how you feel when you say your affirmations. For the best results, consider looking in the direction of "belief" when you say them. The more you say your affirmations, the more natural *and possible* saying them will feel.

The First T: Talk Nice to Yourself!

One of the most meaningful things you can do to reduce your stress and improve the quality of your life is talk nice to yourself. Even so, many people have asked me why I'm suggesting that they do something as "crazy" as talk to themselves.

When I mention "talk nice to yourself" to adults in America, here's the response I get: "I don't talk to myself. I'm a professional!"

(OK... I believe you.)

Now may I ask you a question?

Do you remember the last time you locked your keys in the car?

(I thought you could.)

When I ask that question in my seminars, a large portion of the audience hang their heads and groan.

We've all been through this experience. When I mention it, most people can remember every detail because the scenario is a typical one. It might even have happened something like this:

It's a stressful day to begin with, like a Tuesday after a holiday. You already know what's in store for you. You're going to pay for that holiday you took. Specifically, you've got four days in which to do five days worth of work.

You're almost finished with the details of a big project that you've been working on for weeks. You've got all this paperwork—45 copies of a 15 page report. You've got to present it at 9:00 a.m. to supervisors and co-workers, and this could be your big break. You've put time and energy into it and you're really excited about it. Maybe you're even a little scared, too, because it's such a big deal. You're a trained professional, though, and you're ready to give it all you've got.

You start the night before to give yourself a head start on your big day. You get all the paperwork together and put it neatly on the front seat of your car, eliminating any chance that you'll forget it. You lay out your best outfit, the one you've just had dry cleaned, and do your best to get a good night's sleep.

Unfortunately, you don't get much sleep.

When the alarm goes off in the morning, you get up on the wrong side of the bed. Even though you manage to get into all of your clothes, when you check yourself out in the mirror, you realize this is no longer your best outfit. It's not good enough. You've got to be perfect!

So you pull out every article of clothing you own- shoes, coats, skirts, shirts, blouses, slacks—everything. You finally manage to put together *the* outfit, and you run downstairs to get some coffee before you rush out the door.

In your haste, you spill your coffee—*all over* your great outfit. You have to run back upstairs to put back on your *second best* outfit.

You manage to get dressed (for the third time this morning) and bolt out of the door without your coffee. Now, you're really running late. You speed out to the freeway— swearing and praying at the same time—on the lookout for the police who always seem to notice you at the least opportune moment.

The traffic gods are with you and you screech into your workplace parking lot on two wheels.

Might I mention that two wheels is great for stunt car drivers, but it doesn't do a thing for all those papers that used to be piled so neatly on the front seat of your car. They are now on the floorboards. (Let's not discuss how long it's been since you cleaned out your car.)

At this point, you're trying desperately to breathe. This is a good idea, because your chest seems to have completely locked up.

You get out of the car, lock the door and slam it. On your way to the other side, you happen to look down and notice that your shoes don't match. They're the same color, just two different *styles*. You're struggling to maintain any semblance of coherence at this point. You *yank* open the passenger side door, lay your keys down on the seat, scoop up those papers as efficiently as you can, stand up, lock the door, and slam the door. You take a few steps towards the building... and realize, to your dismay, that you...have locked...your keys...in the car!

Let's pause here for a moment, so I can ask you a very important question.

When you find yourself in a situation like this, what's the first thing you say to yourself?

"Stupid!!!!"

That's not so bad. It was kind of stupid to lock those keys in the car. You had them right on the seat.

"Idiot!!!!"

OK, I'll grant you that anyone with half a brain in her head would have caught the fact that she needed her keys before she left the car.

But do we stop at stupid?

At idiot?

Not usually.

We say, "You *stupid idiot!!!* You're absolutely useless!!! You never do anything right—you screw up everything!!! You can't even dress right! Nobody loves you! Your *parents* didn't want you! *Your coworkers wait for your sick days!* Just look at what you've done *now!*"
(etc...)

Now think about this.

Are you getting your keys out of the car with this behavior?

Are you getting to your big meeting?

Are you having any *fun*??

(I didn't think so.)

If this scenario seems painfully familiar to you, I want to tell you that you're in good company. Just about everybody I've talked to (including myself) has found themselves in this predicament at least once or twice.

It's quite likely that you missed putting the information about that little item of the whereabouts of the keys into your short term memory. You were experiencing what I call a *stress blackout*.

A stress blackout happens when your short term memory is overloaded. The short term memory is the first place that information enters your brain for storage. When you have too much information coming in at one time, overload occurs. Because there is no more room, critical information fails to make it into your short term memory.

If you think of your long term memory as a huge warehouse containing all of your thoughts and memories, both conscious and unconscious, then your short term memory is the equivalent of a bucket. All of the information in the "warehouse" has been put there a "bucket" at a time. Incidentally, the "bucket" can only handle seven pieces of information at a time (plus or minus three).

When you are extremely overloaded, it's as if your "bucket" is full. Not much information gets in. In fact, information is "spilling over the side." Whatever has fallen out will not get into your long term memory because it never got to stay in the "bucket" long enough to make it to the "warehouse."

This might not be so bad if the details we lose weren't often the *most* critical details—like where we put the keys after we turned off the car!

Actually, it's amazing that we manage to do all the things we do. It wouldn't be so bad if those little details we overlooked didn't cause us the most inconvenience when we're the least prepared to deal with it.

Slinging verbal abuse only adds insult to injury.

Unfortunately, many of us save this rough behavior for ourselves. When it comes to other people, we couldn't be nicer.

How would the scenario play out if, instead of you, someone that you really love had locked *their* keys in the car?

Now this isn't just anybody. This is the one person in the world for whom you would do anything, go anywhere, buy anything, try to *be* anything, just because they needed it.

This is the person for whom you would face death itself if the circumstances called for it. This is the person for whom nothing is too great a request.

Imagine for a moment what would happen if *this* person had just gone through the kind of morning I described earlier.

There's your dear friend, standing in the parking lot. Papers scattered on the ground around her feet. She's screaming at herself for screwing up. Other people are giving her a wide berth as they pass on their way in to work. None of them want to receive the kind of verbal abuse that she is giving herself.

You, on the other hand, have the day off. You're sitting in your kitchen, watching your favorite morning news show, lingering over a cup of delicious coffee. You're in your bathrobe and bunny slippers. You haven't bathed yet. You haven't brushed your teeth. You're just enjoying a leisurely, messy, carefree morning.

It's at this point that your internal alarm goes off.

What alarm? It's the alarm that many of us have, usually located in your solar plexus, that alerts you to any danger that may threaten the people that you love. It's the one that goes off in your gut when you have a funny feeling that you should call home and check on the kids, or contact that friend you can't stop thinking about.

If you've got one, you know it often goes off when we have nothing else on our mind—for the moment.

"Rrrinng! Rrrinngg!—Rrrinnng! Somebody I love is in trouble!"

"Gotta help 'em! Gotta find 'em! Gotta save 'em! Gotta *fix it!"*

You jump in your car without a thought of how you look. You cruise the city streets with your emotional radar on full blast, searching for your friend.

You cross traffic illegally without a thought to the police. You go up the wrong way on a one-way street honking your horn at the people who are honking at *you.*

You spot your friend across four lanes of high speed traffic. You make your way across, screech into the parking lot, jump out of the car, and run over to her.

What's the *first* thing you say?

If you're like most people, the first thing you say is nothing like what you would say to yourself. It's also nothing like what your friend is saying to herself.

Most likely, you say, "It's OK, sweetie! I'm here. Everything's going to be all right! Let me get those papers for you. Don't worry about those shoes—if *you* didn't notice them, nobody else will either."

Then you pat her shoulder and say, "Don't you worry about a thing. I'm *right* here. I'll take care of everything."

You can remember yourself doing that very thing, can't you?

117

(Never mind that you haven't had your bath or combed your hair. Never mind that you're in your bathrobe and bunny slippers.)

You put one arm around your friend. In your other arm, you've got all of her papers, all neatly organized. You march right into the front of the building with your friend in tow and a look of determination on your face.

Your expression lets everyone who dares to stare know that this is *your* friend, *you* are in charge, and they had better back off, and let you get on with your business.

You get your friend to the conference room, hunt up a cup of coffee for her, and give her a wink and a "thumbs up" for her meeting.

Now that you've taken care of your friend, you look for someone to get the keys out of her car. Out in the parking lot, you find someone who looks just the type.

You say, "Hey, buddy! Can you break into a car?"

His reply is a bit-too-eager, *"Yeah!"*

You ask your new friend, the break-in professional, to wait for a moment.

You go back into the building to gather your old friend and all the other people from the conference room. You have them follow you out to the parking lot.

While your new buddy is successfully breaking into your friend's car, you open up the trunk of your own car. What have you got in there?

Much to the amazement of the assembled masses, you produce fresh, hot coffee from a special trunk percolator. There are enough ceramic mugs for everyone. You've got doughnuts, you've got balloons, you've got confetti!

You have saved the day. You got your friend's keys out of the car. You got her to her meeting. Everyone has a great time— because of *you.*

You've just made their day! You're still in your bathrobe.

Far from being unusual, this is what we do for other people. With no thought for ourselves, we forge ahead and do whatever it takes to make the lives of people we care about more pleasant.

Bathrobe. Bunny slippers. Whatever it takes.

Now, let's get back to that strategy we were addressing in the first place—talking nice to ourselves. The secret is understanding that what we do without hesitation for the people that we love is exactly what we need to do for ourselves.

We already know that our friendship gives our friends an advantage. With our help, they're *unstoppable.* When they have *us* on their team, our loved ones get encouragement and support in all their endeavors, no matter what it costs us to give it.

The secret of "talk nice to yourself" is to act as if you are your own best friend.

When we choose to do this, then we, too, can become just as unstoppable, unshakable, and unbeatable as the friends we encourage. More than that, we gain an inner strength that makes it easier to support others in positive ways.

As we move closer to the 21st century, we need all the strength we can get. We're already exposed to enough verbal abuse in the world. We don't need to add to the violence by beating *ourselves* up from the inside out.

The world continues to get more complicated. Most of the time, there's little we can do about the negative circumstances we encounter. We can do even less about other people's attitudes. Despite that, there is one thing we can do something about.

We can do something about the way we treat ourselves.

We've already demonstrated how good we are at taking care of others. It's not that much of a stretch, behaviorally, to start taking better care of ourselves. All it takes is a little of the behavior that we're already using on everybody else.

The key to making this change in behavior is understanding the following important statement:

> *Your body responds to a verbal blow in exactly the same way that it responds to a physical blow.*

When you are attacked from the outside, your body responds with the "fight or flight" response. The good news here is that, no matter what the odds, you have a chance to defend yourself. When you're beating yourself up on the inside, you (and your body) have no place to escape. The bad news in this case is that you're stuck—because your tormenter is inside of you.

When you constantly incite the stress response from the inside, you deny yourself critical recovery time. You quickly fall into a state of exhaustion.

How about something completely different?

Up to this point, we've discussed the things we do *for* other people and the things we do *to* ourselves. This first strategy involves an increase in the positive things we do *for* ourselves. All you have to do is to replace the negative words you say to yourself with the positive ones that you say to other people.

This process involves three steps. First, you identify what you say to yourself. Then you identify what you say to other people in the same circumstances. Finally, you choose to replace the former with the latter.

It's been my experience that when you plan this out ahead of time, it's much easier to do it. When you're upset and angry—in the middle of it—you can hardly *think,* much less plan. This process works the same as having fire drills at your house. You have the drills before a fire ever happens. If it ever does, you don't have to think—you do what you you've trained yourself to do. Just as in true emergencies, in "emotional emergencies," we do what we know, not something new.

I encourage you to practice this strategy when you're comfortable and relaxed. Make it a habit that you can count on in an emotional emergency. That way, you'll have it when you need it the most.

Every time you use your new behavior in an emotional emergency, it will become easier to do. It won't be long before you'll find that this new behavior has become second nature to you. You might even be amazed at the results!

The Strategy: Part One

I learned this strategy from Dr. Dan Adams. He was my clinical supervisor at the NAS Chase Field Counseling Center, in Beeville, Texas.

It was 1985. Dr. Dan had noticed that I was often very hard on myself. In the language that I used when referring to myself or in commenting on my own faults, I seemed to have little compassion. Although my compassion and concern for my clients was obvious to him, he was certain that I'd be no good to anyone as a counselor if I couldn't be good to myself first.

His remedy was the strategy that I have used ever since. Here's what he taught me:

1. Get a 3x5 index card and a pencil with a good eraser. Write a note to a someone that you dearly love, in pencil on the card. Since this is the first time, you might want to use

this format:

> Dear _____,
> Thank you for being my friend. The things I
> love about you the most are: _____
>
> _____
>
> _____
>
> I love you!
> (Sign your name)

2. After you've finished writing the letter, go up to the top of the card where you've written your friend's name. Use the eraser to erase his or her name. Write your own name in its place.

Even though this might seem a little silly, writing your name on the index card is your first step in implementing this strategy of learning to talk nice to yourself.

You might find it hard to believe that you are the same kind of person as your friend. That's OK, for now.

Oddly enough, chances are good that the things you admire about your friends are the same qualities you possess, in some measure, yourself. Even if you don't think you possess them, it's likely that these are qualities you would *like* to possess.

It is human nature to recognize what's familiar. If our friends were really all that different from us, we might not have enough in common with them to be friends

3. Now that you've changed the name on the card to your own, your next step is to read the card to yourself. You can start quietly, at first, then read it to yourself out loud. Do this as often as necessary for the next day or so. Keep doing it until you feel more comfortable with it.

Then do it some more.

For even better results, post copies of this index card all around your home—on the bathroom mirror, by the front door, over the light switches in the bedroom. Be creative!

Dr. Dan made me post several copies of this card in my office. This wouldn't have been so bad if it weren't the office where I was seeing clients!

Strangely enough, it was much less embarrassing than I expected. In fact, the experience was quite healing. One of the benefits was the effect that my doing it had on my clients. They could see quite clearly that I was willing to work my own program of recovery, right in front of them. It gave me extra credibility when I offered them the opportunity to try a program of recovery for themselves.

Even so, it took me a couple of weeks to stop feeling stupid about it. It wasn't just the cards that made me feel stupid. I did that quite easily, all by myself.

Dr. Dan made sure I had cards everywhere. I had a card over the light switch, so I saw it every time I went in or out of my office. I had one on my desk, so that no matter what I was working on, it was in my line of sight. I had one on the wall above my desk, so when I looked up it was right in front of me. And I had one in my pocket at all times.

I don't need those cards anymore. All the words I read to myself from those cards finally made it into my conscious mind. These days I use those words without thinking, now they are a part of me.

An extra benefit of this process is that you don't have to believe what you're saying for it to work. Remember, your body doesn't know the difference between what is actually happening and what you imagine. Everything that you say to yourself is accepted by your mind as if it were true. It's up to you to choose what you want to say.

Doing this exercise made me realize how important it is to consider what you choose to say to yourself. Whether it is positive or negative, it will have a direct effect on your self-esteem.

Now that you know about Dr. Dan's strategy, here's one that takes it a step further. My best friend Maggie and I created it by accident. Even so, it still works wonders.

First I'll tell you how it works, then I'll tell you how we created it.

Get another 3x5 card, to write another note to your friend This time, though, you write the words of comfort and encouragement that you would say to them if they made a mistake or had done something that they were upset about. You can use the example on the next page to get started. (Feel free to use both sides of the card.)

Dear _____,

_____

_____

_____

_____

With All My Love, Your Friend,

_____

Once again, when you've finished writing the note to your friend, go ahead and erase his or her name. Write your own name in its place.

Just as you did before, once your name is at the top, read the card to yourself, first quietly, then out loud.

Pay attention to how you feel. Pay attention to any rebuttals that you may want to add to this. If you've been yelling at yourself for a very long time, this may feel *extremely uncomfortable*. That's OK.

It may be useful to keep these cards with you for the next few weeks. Be as patient as possible with yourself.

The more you read these words to yourself, the less uncomfortable it will feel to hear them.

Sooner or later, a situation will arise where you will need to use this new skill you've been practicing. Surprise yourself with positive words. The results can be worth every bit of the effort you've made.

The next time you find yourself starting to call yourself names for any reason, stop right there. Breathe. Then say to yourself the words you've been practicing from your index cards. You can even read from the cards if you want to.

Say the words gently to yourself. Do it several times, if that's what it takes. Feel what it feels like to hear those comforting words, just when you need them the most.

Every time you use this strategy, it becomes easier to use again. Before you know it, you won't need your index cards.

To strengthen this strategy even more, start by saying your comforting words as you look at yourself in the mirror. You can also audio tape yourself saying the words out loud. Play the tape and listen. The more you experiment, the more ways you can discover for using this strategy.

At some point, you will realize that you only speak to yourself in this encouraging and supportive manner. Talking to yourself in this way can have a remarkable effect on your ability to handle any other challenge that you may face.

A Twist on this Strategy

Maggie and I had been best friends for about three years when Dr. Dan taught me about the index cards. She and I were discussing the difficulties of "talking nice" to yourself. We laughed about it, as I remember, because we had spent the last three years talking to each other the way Dr. Dan wanted me to talk to myself!

We both started using those index cards and we got

some good results. However, when things got really difficult for either of us, we found ourselves going back to the
habit of beating ourselves up. It was sometime later, maybe
a year, when we came up with our idea. (Each one of us, to
this day, credits the other one for coming up with it)

We discovered that it was difficult, when we were in the
middle of something that made us really angry or really upset, to come up with something our friend would say. The
instinct for self abuse was too strong within us then.

We did, however, come up with a twist to this strategy.
In a conversation one day, we took this "talking nice" business one step further.

Since we weren't having any luck coming up with each
other's words when we were stressed, we thought we'd try
pretending to *be* one another at that moment, and see if that
made a difference. We were overjoyed to find out that it
did.

The minute we heard our own negative self-talk, we
imagined that we had instantly switched brains with each
other. Inside our heads, we could see the other one's face,
feel what it would feel like if she was with us, and hear the
words she would say *in her voice*. We simply made up a
mental technique to soothe ourselves—and it worked.

We didn't share this technique with anyone else. We figured that we were just being silly. Even though it worked
for us, it was probably too weird to tell people about.

When I started teaching my *Stress Busters* workshops at
Charter Hospital in 1988, I couldn't think of a better way to
explain how this technique worked than to tell people about
our experience. By then it didn't matter if people thought it
was weird. The funny thing about it, though, is that nobody
did.

Affirmations for "Talk Nice to Yourself"

* *I am willing to consider using more positive language with myself.*

* *I am willing to practice using more positive language with myself, starting today.*

* *I deserve to be spoken to in a positive and affirming way. That's how I talk to myself.*

* *I choose to treat myself with respect by speaking to myself in a positive way.*

* *I choose to believe that I am a valuable person. I treat myself that way and I invite others to treat me that way, too. I treat other people with the love and respect that I use on myself.*

Write your own affirmations below:

Workpage—Talk Nice to Yourself!

Document your experiences with these affirmations in the following spaces. Feel free to copy these questions and use them in your journal, or on separate pieces of paper.

1. Here's what happened today:

2. Here's what I said to myself:

3. When I said that to myself, I felt:

4. For me, the results of using this strategy are:

5. The next time I face a similar situation, I'll:

The Second T: Take the Positive

When I suggest "taking the positive" to people in my seminars across the country, I often hear the comment: "What's wrong with you? Don't you watch the news? This is *not* a very positive world we're living in!"

Many of us watch the news or read the paper in the morning or the evening. Most of the stories that make the headlines are about disasters or wars or the criminal activities of public figures. Chances are, it's not news unless it's negative.

If we listen to the radio on the way to work, we hear more of "the news" in between commercials for headaches, stomach aches, hemorrhoids, constipation, lower back pain, and any number of other complaints. That we manage to get to work at all without pulling off to the side of the road in a state of complete depression is testament to our strength of character!

During the workday, we hear how sales are slipping, prices are down, layoffs are imminent, production is suffering, morale is low. Add to this the personal interactions with supervisors or co-workers who remind us of our deficiencies on a regular basis.

When we get home, our family members or room mates will have more problems and complaints for us to deal with. We're only too ready to let *them* have a dose of what *we've* been putting up with all day.

By the time we get to bed at night, the only break we

may have gotten from all the negativity was the sitcom in which the boss is a fool and the next door neighbor got his just desserts when the kids left their skateboard in his driveway.

I have an alternative that works wonders for reducing your stress levels.

What would happen if you decided to miss the news, or if you only read the comics and the sports section on a regular basis? My mother tells me that watching *Sesame Street* on PBS every day has kept her stress levels low for years!

Better yet, when you choose to read the news, what would happen if you considered what happens in "real life" once the cameras stop rolling and the reporters have left? There's always more than meets the eye. There's more to the world than what they can tell you in the micro-stories of the news.

Once you take a look beyond the headlines, you will find stories of bravery and heroism and caring and friendship. When you consider them in this light, the stories are much more positive—many of them invite celebration!

For instance, you probably haven't heard about those people on that bridge that collapsed in San Francisco who became best friends because of what they survived together. They get together with their families and other friends every year on the anniversary of the day they met—and celebrate life.

You probably also missed the significance of the wedding announcement of two other disaster survivors about a year after their apartment building collapsed during an earthquake. It turns out that the man lived upstairs and the woman lived downstairs They met and fell in love after his apartment crashed down into hers. Until then, they had never met—even though they had both lived in the same building for years. They figured it was fate. They smile when they describe how they met.

When we hear about disasters on TV, we shake our heads and think, "How awful!" That's because we never hear the *rest of the story*. Wouldn't you think about disasters in a different light if you considered that every disaster contains the seeds of some miracle?

For example, Mothers Against Drunk Driving, or the work that Len Bias' mother is doing educating kids about drugs, or even the spotlight the late Barbara Glaser put on children with AIDS because of her own tragedy. These are all miracles born out of catastrophe and grief and pain.

We think of these people as heroes, as having something special that the rest of us don't have. Maybe they do. And maybe they simply chose to believe that they could create a miracle out of their own personal disaster.

Maybe we're more like them than we know.

Think about it. Think about the things you have survived in your lifetime—the grief, the pain, the crises. At the time, you might have thought that you would never get through it, but you did—with prayer, with patience, with the help of good friends. Maybe all you needed was the passing of time.

The skills and knowledge you have today, the compassion you have for others, the perspective that you have—can't you trace them back to the time you developed them? Nine times out of ten, it was in difficult times.

Five years from now, you're going to be so proud of yourself for getting through the difficulties you're experiencing now. You're going to see how much you grew as you handled each obstacle that you faced. You're going to be very aware of how significant the difficulties were in the overall scheme of your life. It will feel really good—you may even congratulate yourself when you think about it.

I say, why wait five years? Congratulate yourself now, even though you might not feel like it. Give yourself a five year head start your future celebrations. You're learning something important here, and celebrating the positive, in spite of the negative, is a powerful stress reducer.

Why? Because the idea of positive and negative are *constructs*—something we use to make sense of what's happening in the world around us. What is positive, anyway, and what is negative? How can you tell?

You've already discovered that your brain does not distinguish between the real and the imagined. It doesn't distinguish between positive and negative circumstances, either. It only responds to the meaning that you give to what happens to you. Deciding what meaning you will give to your circumstances is your choice.

Nothing brings this point home to me better than the stories of the people who came out of the concentration camps and POW camps after World War II and Korea.

Research done at the time by a psychologist named Julian Rotter indicated that people who survived the camps gave one of two meanings to their experience. It's evident from his work that the people who survived were affected much more by the meaning they gave to their experiences than by the experience itself.

For instance, some of the survivors came out of the camps as broken people. It was as if their spirits had been crushed, and only their bodies had survived. These people were the ones who believed, "If they can do this to me, what other terrible things could happen? What's the use— I'm at the mercy of circumstances. There's nothing I can do." Their experience had been one of loss and defeat.

Even so, there was another kind of person who survived the same circumstances. These were the ones who, once freed, went on to make a great difference in their communities; some of them, in the world. They seemed to have come out of their experience bigger than they had been when they went in—more full of life. They seemed to have the feeling that they had some great purpose to fulfill for humanity. They believed, "If I can survive *that*, I can survive anything! There's a reason for me to be alive. I am responsible for what I do with the rest of my life so that my experience will have meaning for the people whose lives I will touch. I can accomplish anything!"

It's incredible to imagine that the only difference in their response was the meaning they gave to what they'd been through, but it's true.

Believe it or not, you and I are no different, even though some of us are better at this than others. It's never too late to decide to "take the positive." What's the worst thing that can happen? If we're mistaken, at least it makes the road a lot easier to travel. And if it really is true, *Wow!* The possibilities for improving your life and reducing your stress are endless.

Of course, learning to "take the positive" is a process. I had to learn it, too. For the most part, I first learned it from stories I heard other people tell. That's how I found out what was possible. After I got the hang of it, I created my own learning experiences.

The stories that follow are two that I heard early in my own progress in the direction of positive thinking. These are still my two favorites, and I use them often when I teach.

This first one is a story that I heard so many years ago, I've lost all memory of where. As far as I'm concerned, though, the story itself is unforgettable.

Since I first heard it, I've come across variations of the

details, but the point is always the same. Here, then, is my version:

There was once an old man who lived in a small village in feudal China. He lived in a shack, had little food and even fewer possessions.

Despite his meager circumstances, he seemed quite content. He always had a kind word for everyone he met.

He had two things in the world that he treasured above all else: his only son, and a horse that a nobleman had given him as a reward for a kind deed.

One day, the horse and the boy were out riding in the countryside. In the course of the ride, the horse became frightened, reared up, and threw the boy off his back. The boy broke both of his legs in the fall.

When the horse returned to the village alone, a search party was sent out. Neighbors of the old man soon found the boy and went running to his shack to tell him of the tragedy.

"Come quickly! Something *terrible* has happened! Your son is near death. He's broken both of his legs while riding that nobleman's horse. It's such a tragedy. We're so sorry for you!!"

The old man remained calm. He said quietly "Take me to my son."

His neighbors couldn't believe it. As far as they were concerned, this was a disaster. There were no doctors, no hospitals. If the boy survived, the best he could hope for was to walk with a limp. The neighbors shook their heads and clicked their tongues.

When he got to the boy, the old man set the broken legs and carried his son back home. Despite the circumstances, he maintained his usual calm demeanor.

Later in the day, as the old man was grooming the

horse and talking to it outside of his house, some of his neighbors came up to him and shook their fists in his face.

"Have you no heart?," they yelled. "Your son lies crippled inside and you haven't even shed a tear. You're treating this evil horse as if no harm had been done to your boy. You don't even look upset. What's wrong with you?"

The old man looked up at his neighbors. Calmly he said, "How do you know that what has happened is bad?"

The people were stunned; they went away shaking their heads and muttering.

Three days later, the emperor's army came through town to conscript soldiers for the coming wars. No villager who left with them would ever be seen again. They took every male in the village, 12 years old or older, leaving only the old men, the women, and the children.

The only young man who was not taken was the boy with the two broken legs. His legs would heal, and the old man did not lose his son.

That story has always put things in perspective for me—who's to say what's positive? Psychologists have suggested that we describe reality in ways that make sense to us. Our descriptions are nothing more than that: descriptions.

Albert Ellis, in his book, *A New Guide to Rational Living,* suggests that we do not respond to what is actually happening, we respond to what we *tell* ourselves is happening. We can change our response to what we've called stressful situations, by changing our descriptions.

When I think about changing descriptions, also known as "reframing," I can think of no better story to explain it than this next one. I even remember where I heard it first.

I was working as a counselor in the Navy when I was introduced to the work of Fr. Joseph Martin. Father Martin is a Jesuit priest, and a recovering alcoholic. His "mission" is to carry the message of recovery to those persons still suffering from the disease of alcoholism. Father Martin is also a wonderful speaker and a great storyteller. One of the first stories I ever heard him tell was this one, about this process of reframing. Here's my version of it:

Once upon a time, there were two little boys who lived in the same town. Both of them were famous. One was famous for being a perfect pessimist; the other was famous for being a perfect optimist. What made these boys even more famous was the fact that the pessimist came from the wealthiest family in town, and the optimist came from the poorest family in town.

One day, when the boys were about eight years old, a team of psychologists came to town to try to determine the reasons behind the boys' behavior.

With permission from the boys' parents, the psychologists set up an experiment.

First, they took the pessimist to the biggest shopping mall in town. They had reserved it for the entire day for the purposes of their experiment. They had shipped in extra toys and candy, video games, and a huge merry go round. On this day, the entire mall was filled with everything a kid could want to look at, eat, play with, or own.

The psychologists brought the pessimistic boy into the middle of the mall. They said, "Son, everything in this mall is yours until we come back. You can touch everything, play with anything, eat anything you want. If you see anything you'd like to take home with you, it's yours, with our compliments.

"This entire mall is empty of people and we'll be

right outside the mall entrance so you are completely safe. We'll be back in a couple of hours—so go ahead and have all the fun you want!"

Four hours later the psychologists came back. They found the pessimistic boy sitting on the bench where they'd left him. He was looking at the floor. He didn't appear to have moved from that spot for the entire time he'd been there.

The psychologists said, "Son, have you had any fun?"

The boy said, "No, sir, I didn't want to get dirty."

"Did you play with anything?"

"No, sir, I didn't want to break anything."

"Did you have anything to eat?"

"No, sir, I didn't want to stain my clothes."

"Is there anything here that you want?"

"No, sir, I didn't want to choose the wrong thing. Can I please go home now?"

So they took him back to his parents and made notations in their scientific notebooks.

Meanwhile, on the other side of town, other members of the team were setting up an experiment with the optimistic boy. For him, they had found the biggest barn in the countryside. They filled it, floor to ceiling, with fresh horse manure.

There was a space just inside the door, about 6' by 6', where the boy could move around. There were some farm implements hanging on the wall. Other than that, the entire area was pure manure.

The psychologists brought the smiling boy into the barn. "Son," they said, "we'd like you to help us out today. We're going to leave you in here for a very short while and then we'll come back in and get you. We won't be far away and you'll be completely safe in here. You can do whatever you like. We'll be back real soon. OK?"

"OK!," said the boy, who was eager to see what would happen next.

Four hours later, the psychologists returned. Before they reached the door of the barn, they heard a rhythmic scraping sound and loud, off-key singing coming from inside.

When they opened the door to look, the boy was nowhere in sight. All they could see was an uneven path through the middle of the manure— and shovels full of the brown stuff flying toward the doorway where they stood.

"Hey, kid," one of the psychologists yelled. "What are you doing?"

The kid yelled back, "I'm diggin'!"

"Why?", yelled the psychologists.

"I know with all this manure in here, there's *got* to be a pony!"

I *still* laugh at that story. It certainly puts things in perspective, hmm?

That story has gotten me through some rough times and helped me to reframe my circumstances when I really needed to the most.

When I suggest that you "take the positive," it's just my way of saying, "keep digging for that pony."

So take the positive—and here are some exercises to help you start the process. Before you know it, positive self talk can be as much a part of you as your name.

Exercise #1: Paying Attention to your Language.

Have you ever considered the difference between the percentage of positive and negative words in the English language? When you think about it, do you notice that we have at least twice as many negative words—not to mention ideas—as we have positive ones?

The reasons for this are simple. By the time you finish this exercise, you will probably have figured it out for yourself.

First things first, though. Let's talk about the words you use on a regular basis. Make a list of all the descriptive words that you can think of, and list them below, or on a separate piece of paper. Go ahead, try it...

(To get the best results out of this exercise, make your list before you read any further.)

List of descriptive words:

How many of your descriptive words are positive?

If the total number of positive words in your list is 50% or more, then you're well on your way to being able to start practicing the strategy of "take the positive."

If the number of positive words in your list is less than 50%, you may want to increase the amount of positive words in your vocabulary before you tackle the prospect of practicing this strategy.

Why? Without the words with which to describe the positive, it's very hard to experience it.

(No problem, though—because, as usual, I have a plan!)

If you would like to begin using more positive words than you do now, the first place to start is with a dictionary. I've invented a little exercise that works wonders for increasing the number of positive words at your disposal. Once again, try this at your own pace. You may be pleasantly surprised at how much fun you can have.

Exercise #2: Using the Dictionary

Find the positive words in your list above. (In the unlikely event that you have listed no positive words—think of some right now and look those up!)

You might find it useful to write down your words on a separate piece of paper, or in your journal. One at a time, look those words up in your dictionary.

Next to each word, write down the dictionary description, or paraphrase it in your own words.

Now that you have written down the word and its description(s), take a few moments to read them to yourself.

Have you found a gold mine of positive words? Chances are that you have. Did you look up the other words that were listed as synonyms? Doing that is even more exciting.

Once you've finished reading your definitions to yourself, you're ready to add the most significant piece to this process.

For each word that you have listed, write down a summary of a time when you actually experienced this feeling, this state of being, this adjective. If you have listed words that you have never experienced, now's your chance to conduct some field research! Give yourself the opportunity to experience them by planning the circumstances in which you will. Then you can come back and finish this exercise.

Now take a few moments to enjoy the feelings you experience.

You can do this on a regular basis, or anytime you feel like it. The more you do it, the easier it becomes to remember your positive qualities in the midst of negative circumstances! When you're feeling positive about yourself and your abilities, it's so much easier to "Take the positive" in challenging circumstances.

Just to show you how easy it is, let's try working through it once. (I've got a great word...)

Step One: Write down the word.

Brilliant

Step Two: Write the definition(s) that matter to you (In this case, I left out definitions 2 and 3). You can also paraphrase if you would prefer.

adj. 1. Full of light, shining. (See synonyms at bright)...4. Glorious, magnificent. 5. Superb, wonderful. 6. Marked by unusual and impressive intellectual acuteness. (See synonyms at intelligent)

In this case, the word I chose is also a noun. I added that definition, too.

n. A precious gem, especially a diamond, finely cut in any of various forms with numerous facets.

Step Three: Write an example of experiencing this feeling, this state of being, this adjective.

As I was writing the Four T's for *Pizza and the Art of Life Management,* I was trying to think of a good exercise to help me explain the process of positive thinking.

As I considered the mental "tricks" I use on myself, this idea of how I use the dictionary flashed across my brain. "Yes! That's it!"

As I quickly wrote down my strategy of looking up the words that described my mental pictures, I felt so good, so strongly good, that this exercise was going to make a lot of people smile. It felt so brightly brilliant, so great to be a part of it, that I had to laugh out loud in gratitude for the idea.

Step Four: Feel how it feels to experience what you've written about yourself.

Thank you!

How was that?

It might have been exhilarating, interesting, or downright uncomfortable. No matter. You're simply experiencing your own starting point. Keep doing it, be gentle with yourself, and track your progress.

Just like you would if you were exercising any muscle, you'll get better at this with practice. Pretty soon it won't hurt a bit, and you can look forward to the practice with enthusiasm. You'll also feel so much better afterwards.

Why this it so challenging for some of us?

I don't know about you, but I can tell you why it was challenging for me when I first began to practice the process.

Every time I said something positive about myself, my whole body denied it. My brain cried out "That's a *lie!*" I had believed for so long that I was "despicable" that my brain would not accept any information that suggested otherwise.

Like many of the people I've heard from over the years, I simply could not imagine what was so darn positive. Life was hard, and that was that.

Like many people, I got so used to this general atmosphere of negativity that if someone gave me a compliment, my first response was, "What do you want, money?" If a co-worker thanked me for helping them out on a big project, I'd say "Don't worry about it. It was nothing." And if someone at work admired my outfit, I'd say "This old thing? I just got it out of the laundry."

When this is the environment we have lived in for years, the suggestion that we could "take the positive" might pose quite a challenge. Like me, all those years ago, you might think that there isn't enough positive in your life to even *notice*, let alone take.

Overcoming years of negative conditioning takes time.

If you completed the previous exercise, and practice it on a regular basis, you can develop a sense of your own goodness. This knowledge is the armor you can use to defend yourself against any random negativity that you might encounter. Looking for the positive, in people and in circumstances, is the best way to find it!

Exercise #3: Planning for the Positive

It's been my experience that having a plan makes all the difference when you're beginning a course of new behavior.

When I first started focusing on the positive things in the world around me, I had to give up some of the negative behaviors that were keeping me stuck. I was spending so much time reinforcing my negative attitude, there was no room for the positive one to grow.

Somewhere along the way, I developed this strategy. There are five steps to it.

First, take a few moments now to make a list of all the things you can think of that are positive for you, things that you enjoy. (For example: soft guitar music, sunsets, Greek lemon soup, a clean car, etc.) Don't worry about how far-fetched anything you write may seem, just list everything you can think of.

Now that you have a list, go through the items you've listed. Now, start a new list of all the things on your first list that you can reasonably expect to experience today, or in the near future. (This doesn't mean that you are currently experiencing it, only that you don't have to buy something new or travel a great distance to do so.)

You can even include things on your list that you have not taken the time to experience, even though you could if you chose to, with the resources you have right now. Feel free to cheat liberally: if you think of something for this new list that is not on the first one, add it anyway!

Now that you have a list of all the things you can reasonably expect to be able to do, choose *five* of them. These are the five things that you will make a commitment to do in the next seven to ten days. It doesn't matter how small they are or how little time it would take to experience them.

Start simply, and give yourself the opportunity to work up to bigger things.

The five things I will commit to doing in the next seven to ten days are:

1.

2.

3.

4.

5.

Now that you've committed to doing these five things, you have to be sure that you'll have time for them. A simple way to accomplish that is to let go of some of the activities that you currently spend time on that are not as useful to you. For the sake of our discussion, I'll call them negative behaviors.

These are the things that subtract from your life rather than add to it. I'm suggesting that you replace those negative behaviors or activities with the five positive behaviors you have listed above.

For example: if listening to music is one of your choices, then you could choose to listen to a favorite tape in the morning instead of watching the morning news. If you like to read the paper and find that the news depresses or angers you, you could commit to reading the comics instead of hard news. Use your imagination!

I am willing to replace five of my negative behaviors/ activities with five of my positive behaviors/activities.

    1. Instead of _____,

      I will _____.

    2. Instead of _____,

      I will _____.

    3. Instead of _____,

      I will _____.

    4. Instead of _____,

      I will _____.

    5. Instead of _____,

      I will _____.

Now that you have your plan made up, choose which activity you will try first. Whatever you choose, pay attention to how you feel after you practice that positive behavior instead of a negative one. The more you do this, the better prepared you will be to increase the number of your positive choices.

A great way to track your progress is to keep a record of your experiences in your journal. Whether you record it or not, with regular practice this strategy can become a habit. Once you've got the habit of taking the positive despite your circumstances, you'll be amazed at how successfully you can face anything that comes up.

Affirmations for "Take the Positive"

* *I am willing to consider being more positive today.*

* *I am willing to practice one positive behavior today.*

* *I deserve to create a positive environment for myself. I surround myself with positive people, and I pay attention to each positive experience I encounter today.*

* *I choose to believe that the world is a nourishing place and that I am supported by it.*

* *I choose to find the positive in everything I experience today.*

Write your own affirmations below:

Workpage: Take the Positive

Describe a situation in which you choose to be positive today. (Feel free to copy these questions for your personal use.)

What was the situation:

What I did/said to myself:

How that felt:

The results of using this strategy were:

The next time I have to deal with something like this, I'll:

The Third T: Try Smiling

Many people at my workshops laugh at this idea. How can smiling possibly reduce their stress? They've been smiling all their lives, and it hasn't reduced their stress a bit. Of course, when they show you how they've been smiling, you understand why it hasn't worked for them.

They're using that "social" smile, the one we've all been taught to use when we have to put up with someone or something that we don't like. The lips are turned up, you can see the teeth—but the eyes aren't smiling at all.

That kind of smiling doesn't reduce our stress one bit. It's really just a way of biting back your true feelings. In fact, if you do it all the time, you can increase your stress levels significantly.

So when I say "try smiling," what am I talking about?

I'm talking about the kind of smiling you do when you just can't help it. It's the kind of smiling that bursts onto your face when you're happy. When your small son runs up to you with a flower that he just picked for you "special!" and you smile because you can't contain your joy. When your teenage daughter tells you that you were right about something and she *thanks* you. She can fill your heart with so much joy that it lights up your face.

"Delight" is a word that comes close to describing these things.

The presence of delight in our lives is essential for reducing our stress. Delight is one of those emotions that increases our endorphins, Nature's most potent stress reducers.

Delight can be a surprise, or it can be a conscious choice. When you choose to smile—or laugh—you give yourself the gift of delight.

How can this be?

We've already discussed the fact that your body doesn't

know the difference between reality and imagination. When you choose to smile, you give your body the message that something great is happening, and your body can't help but respond as if it were true. It even works if you're pretending!

As a matter of fact, whether you're pretending or not, your response to circumstances has everything to do with the mood you're in and little to do with the circumstances you're facing.

Think about it.

When you're delighted, or just feeling happy, you seem to have the world on a string, doesn't you? When you're in a great mood, there's not much that can get you down, right?

Somebody could come running up to you at work, breathing hard, all upset and say, "They've just hit your car in the parking lot! It looks like a *golf ball.* And they got away!"

If this happened on a day when you're in a great mood—delighted, even—you'd probably just shrug your shoulders and say, "No problem! I've got insurance. I'll get a car I really like!"

But on those days when you're in a bad mood, feeling negative about everything and everyone, you've most likely convinced yourself that nothing good can possibly happen.

When you're in a bad mood, your *whole body* is in a bad mood. You're hunkered down at your desk, you're practically snarling, and nobody wants to come near you.

All of a sudden, some guy comes running up to you, breathing hard, all excited, and he says, "You've just won 40 million dollars in the State Lottery! Congratulations! You're a millionaire!"

How do you respond to *that*? It's your bad mood day today, and you've got an answer for this jerk.

"40 *million* dollars? Do you know how much *tax* I'm

gonna have to pay on that?"

It's not the circumstances. It's your attitude!

Your attitude affects your ability to smile, and your willingness to choose to smile affects your attitude.

Smiling, like breathing, is a semi-voluntary action. Have you ever found yourself smiling despite your best intentions? Because it's semi-voluntary, you can also choose to smile when you don't really feel like it.

At first, you might need a plan to do this. Some of you might even need scientific proof.

Several years ago, I took a social psychology class at a local college and I learned some interesting things about smiling. In addition, I got some scientific confirmation for the idea that smiling reduces stress. Here's what I found out:

Several years ago, there was a group of social psychologists at a University. They wanted to find out if the position of a person's face had anything to do with their mood.

Because they had to isolate only the behavior they were testing for, they had to find subjects who would not be able to move anything but their faces. They found 80 people who, due to various circumstances, were unable to move their arms, legs or bodies. Of the 80 people that they approached, 40 people volunteered to participate in their experiment.

The psychologists told the volunteers that they were working on a computer and stylus combination which would enable people with disabilities to join the work force. (Fortunately, this was also true.) What they needed from their subjects was help in deciding the best way to hold the stylus, considering that it had to be held by mouth instead of by hand.

The psychologists divided the volunteers into three groups. Each group was seated in exactly the same kind of environment, had exactly the same kind of computer, ran through exactly the same exercises, spent exactly the same amount of time. Everything was identical, except one thing.

The only difference from group to group was the way in which the volunteers held the stylus.

The first group was told to hold the stylus like they would hold a cigarette—loosely, right in the middle of their lips. The second group was told to hold it in their teeth, tightly, without using their lips. The third group was told to hold it tightly in their lips, without using their teeth.

After the experiment was over, one of the psychologists went into each of the three classrooms to congratulate the volunteers and thank them for all their hard work. He told them that the experiment was concluded, and that their families and assistants were waiting to escort them home. He told them that one of his colleagues would meet them at the outside door in case they had any questions on their way out.

He assured them that they would be notified of the results of the experiment as soon as all the data had been analyzed. They could expect to be brought back to the center and trained with the stylus in the way that proved to be most effective. In the meantime, they were free to go.

The first group that came out was the group that had held the stylus like a cigarette, loosely in their lips. They came out quietly and were wheeled to the door which led outside.

The psychologist at the front door asked them, as a group, if there were any questions.

"Nope."

Were there any problems?

"Nope."

The psychologist thanked them and wished them a nice day.

"Yup."

The second group arrived with their escorts shortly afterwards. These were the volunteers who had held the stylus in their teeth. As a whole, they were making a lot of noise.

One of them was yelling about wood chips in his teeth, others were yelling about the ridiculous experiment and all the stupid people here. Another was threatening legal action to anyone who would listen, yelling that he never wanted to be contacted again. This was not a happy group.

The psychologist who was stationed at the door heard this group coming before he saw them. This was not a group with whom he wanted interact. For protection, he stood with his back to them and pretended to be studying a picture on the wall. The group left the building, yelling at (and to) one another and the escorts all the way to the parking lot. They didn't even notice the man by the wall.

The third group never came out of their classroom.

After about 10 minutes, the psychologist who had been waiting at the door poked his face into their room. He was amazed at what he saw.

All of the volunteers were still in their places, laughing and talking. Every one of them appeared to be having a great time.

One was commenting on the success of the experiment and how she hoped that their group would be back together again very soon. One man was exclaiming to a woman in his aisle that they were neighbors and would really have to get together again, maybe for dinner next week, so they could introduce their spouses.

One woman was suggesting a victory party for the group. Another suggested that if they stayed where they were they might be invited to participate in another experiment. It was obvious to the most casual observer that these people were having fun.

What happened to make the experiences of these groups so dissimilar?

The only difference was the position of their faces!

With the help of each group of these volunteers, the social psychologists demonstrated that our emotions are greatly affected by our facial expressions.

This isn't just a scientific experiment reserved for a laboratory; you can try it for yourself. Just read the directions that follow, try maintaining each of the following expressions and take notes on the experience.

1. Try removing all expression from your face and staying like that for one minute. (You can do this with a friend to help you or you can do it in the mirror to see what you look like.) What happens?

2. Try gritting your teeth for one minute. (Many of us have been gritting our teeth, as a habit, for years. We do it all the time and we hardly notice it anymore. For the purpose of this experiment, you can put a pencil in your teeth and bite down hard for one minute, or as long as you can stand it.) What happens?

3. Try holding a pencil (minus the eraser) in your lips, without using your teeth, for one minute. You don't have to use a pencil, though. You could just make what's called a "kissy face." Pucker up your lips. (Noises are optional.) What happens?

What have you discovered about the position of your face and your mood?

Chances are that keeping no expression on your face resulted in a feeling similar to apathy. You may recognize this feeling as the one you have when you're feeling helpless or frustrated because nothing you do seems to make any difference in circumstances at work or with another person. For all practical purposes, it's a "shut down" mode.

Many people have adopted this expression, with its resulting attitude, as the path of least resistance.

The "pencil in your teeth" position may have resulted in a feeling of anger or aggravation. You may have wanted to scream about the wood chips in your teeth, or you may even have been tempted to slap the first person you came across.

Many people have adopted a version of this expression in their daily lives. These are the people who simply won't be cut off in traffic without aiming a gun at your car—and it doesn't even have to be a real weapon. People who yell at you when you say hello, people who have an unkind word for everyone and everything. These people may simply have been biting back so much for so long that it's gotten the best of them. They're carrying around such an overflow of pent-up emotion, it's difficult for them to refrain from taking out their frustrations on everybody.

The "kissy face" position may have looked the silliest, but I'll bet you had the most fun with it. It's hard not to laugh when you're trying to keep that expression on your face. We make that face all the time—to our babies, to our pets, to stranger's children in the supermarket line, to our sweethearts.

Chances are, that face is one we associate with laughter and *fun*.

What would happen if we used it, or a version of it, more often in our daily lives? I wonder what would happen to the state of world affairs if more people knew about this, and used it.

You've already proven to yourself that the position of your face can affect your mood in powerful ways. When you were doing your experiment, you weren't dealing with emotions, you were simply practicing behaviors. Imagine what your world would be like if you chose a behavior that would result in your good mood.

When you think about it, what kind of people do you like to be around? Is it the people who seem to be apathetic all the time, who seem to be angry all the time, or is it the ones who seem to be laughing much of the time?

Maybe one of the benefits those laughing people experience is that they won't be considered serious enough to be in charge of that big committee or project. While the rest of us are working weekends and nights to prove to everyone just how good we are, they're out fishing or spending time with their families.

Consider this: who looks better on Monday morning? Who do you think has more fun in life, the laughers or those serious people with their noses to the grindstone?

Even when you know all of this, and even though you can get really good at this kissy face technique, you may still experience one of those days when it doesn't work. This might be the kind of day when you need more help than you're getting from those pieces of tape holding your smile up. When nothing you do results in the remotest approximation of a smile, that's the time for my "full body smile technique."

The reason you need the full body technique is because when you are having a bad day, your *whole body* is having a bad day. Your shoulders are hunched over, your face is droopy, you're sighing deeply at regular intervals, and nothing seems to cheer you up.

In order to make the best use of this technique, it's important to use it as soon as you recognize your symptoms.

The minute you realize that you're having a *whole body bad day*, you've got to take action. You've got to get yourself, as quickly as possible, to someplace private. This could be an empty conference room, the restroom, or it might be as easy as closing your office door. If you're at home, get to your bedroom, or the bathroom—as long as you're alone and out of sight. (You need to be out of sight to do this because it's kind of weird.)

Now. You're alone, right? OK.

You need to do the next three things in this order: (1) stand up straight with your shoulders back, (2) put your head back, (3) open your mouth—real wide. After a few moments, what happens?

This is so *silly,* you've *got to* crack up!!

When you exit from your hiding place after doing this technique, you'll probably be laughing softly to yourself or even smiling broadly. Most likely, you'll feel a whole lot better than you did before.

If you're at work, you have an added benefit. Anyone who saw you walk into your hiding place, *and* walk out, will notice a huge difference in your demeanor. It will be so marked that they may feel a very strong urge to call Security!

If you think about it, that alone could make it worth trying.

So try smiling—and enjoy the process!

Smiling Exercises

Give yourself an extra boost in your plan to try smiling by knowing what actually makes you smile. The goal here is to inspire yourself to delight on a regular basis, as a supplement to your smiling behavior. I like to think of this as smile vitamins.

As usual, this is a process. Once you get the hang of it, work through it in a way that makes the most sense to you.

Exercise #1: What Makes You Smile?

First, get a piece of paper and make three columns on it. Label one column *visual*, another column *auditory*, and the other column *kinesthetic*. (You can also get three pieces of paper, and label each page as if it were a column.)

The three categories we're using come from a methodology developed in the 1970's by John Bandler and Richard Grinder, as practiced in the system of Neurolinguistic Programming (NLP). (As you may remember, these are the same folks who brought you the "Belief Technique" that I described in the Affirmations section.)

In NLP, these three categories are called Representational Systems. They represent Bandler and Grinder's discovery that we receive our information about the world around us from three general sources. Those sources are:

what we see (visual), what we hear (auditory), and what we sense through our feelings (kinesthetic—as in "feel your way through it").

There is an entire body of knowledge about the use of NLP in developing rapport, and in communicating more effectively with others as well as with yourself. There is a wide range of applications in business, counseling, interpersonal communications, and sports. (The book *Instant Rapport*, by Michael Brooks, is a nice introduction to the basics of NLP. The book *Heart of the Mind*, by Connirae and Steve Andreas, is more advanced. You'll find Information on both books in the Resources section at the end of this book.)

For the sake of our exercise here, I simply want to increase your use of the Representational Systems, so you can get as wide a variety of delightful experiences as you possibly can.

For that reason, I've asked you to make three columns, or use three pages.

In the visual column (page), list all the things that make you smile when you see them.

In the auditory column (page), list all the things that make you smile when you hear them.

In the kinesthetic column (page), list all the things that make you smile when you feel them.

Visual	Auditory	Kinesthetic

Hopefully, this exercise is easy for you. That's *great!*

If you're having a little trouble getting started, let me share with you what's in my columns. The most wonderful feature of this exercise is that, no matter what you put in your columns, there's really no way to make a mistake. It's simply a matter of personal choice.

On my Visual Level: Things that make me smile when I see them:

Pictures: ocean scenes, waterfalls, peaceful lakes, anything with lots of deep blue in it, photos of Chuck, photos of any of my family or friends, written affirmations or positive sayings, etc.

Movies: *The Wizard of OZ, The Neverending Story, Field of Dreams,* The *Star Wars* Trilogy, *Wild Hearts Can't Be Broken, Scrooge, Monty Python and the Holy Grail, Beaches,* etc.

Books: The *Annotated Sherlock Holmes, The Mists of Avalon, The Phantom Tollbooth, Hans Christian Anderson Fairy Tales, Women Who Run with the Wolves,* my journal, etc.

On my Auditory Level: Things that make me smile when I hear them:

Recordings: Traditional Irish music (pipes, flutes, harp, the old ballads), Mozart, classical piano music, my sister Deirdre singing anything, Deirdre's *Lightsisters: Shine On,* jazz piano and saxophone, The Beatles, old comedy recordings from the Sixties, the soundtracks from musicals like *My Fair Lady, Gigi,* and *The Sound of Music,* pre-1980 Neil Young, rock'n'roll from the late 60's and early 70's, etc.

Other sounds: the ocean, a waterfall, wind through the trees, Chuck's voice, my mother's voice—and her laughter, or the voice of anyone I love, the words: "we'd like to hire you for our program", the words "thank you", laughter from anywhere, the sounds of a quiet place, the sound of my own voice singing a song—even if it's off key.

On my Kinesthetic (Feeling) Level: Things that make me feel good when I experience them:

Hugs!, building a fire in the fireplace or at a campsite and then sitting back and enjoying it by myself or with someone I love, Earl Grey tea—hot!-first thing in the morning, legwarmers, exploring places I have never been before, walking in the woods or by the ocean, being alone, sharing with an audience, hot baths in a deep bathtub, goosedown quilts, etc.

Was that fun or what? Just sharing my list with you has me grinning from ear to ear. What was it like for you? Do we share any common joys?

Now, let me ask you a question. If you made a list, how many of your choices are things that you actually allow yourself to experience on a regular basis? The fact is, for this to work, it has to be more than just a list on paper. You have to choose to create more of what brings you delight in your life.

It may be that you've never thought of the things which bring you delight. It's possible that you thought of them a long time ago, and then you got busy and forgot. No matter, you've got your list now—or, at least, a good start on making one.

Once you've created your lists of things that make you smile when you see them, hear them and feel them, the next step is to bring those things into your life on a regular basis. You do this by making the conscious choice to surround yourself with opportunities to experience them. That is, you won't have to look very far to see something that brings you delight. You will be within range of the things that are delightful to hear, and you will be in close proximity to the things that feel good to you.

When I became aware of how useful the things on my list were, I started to use them full time to increase my ability to smile when I needed to the most and felt like it the least. These days, I am never without options for delight.

I make it a point to surround myself with the visual reminders of what brings me joy: there are *lots* of blue things in my home and office because that's the color that makes me smile the most. I have pictures of my loved ones on the walls and on my desk, so I can look into their faces anytime I want. There is always water somewhere near me, whether it's a picture or a place, because it soothes me more than anything when I need a smile. I keep a box of photos and mementos, glowing evaluations from my programs and notes and cards that are uplifting, so I can pull it down and look through it when I need a mental lift. (And, of course, I have that little box of Chinese fortune cookie fortunes that I mentioned in *Bootstrap Words*..)

I keep a pile of my special CD's right near my desk, so I can listen to them while I'm working. The music soothes me when I'm working on something difficult. No matter how much I'm travelling, I'm only a phone call away from all of the people whose voices and laughter make me smile. And I can always sing "It's a Long Way to Tipperary," no matter where I am!

Walking in the woods or near water is something I do three or four times a week Living in beautiful Austin, Texas makes this very easy. I get hugs from Chuck a lot, and I give out hugs to anyone who wants them. Even if I'm all alone I can reach both my arms around myself and get a hug to tide me over. I always have lots of Earl Grey tea on hand, and lots of great smelling things to put in the bathwater. I make it a point to smell things that make me smile wherever I am, even if it's just putting a little perfume on my wrists and temples after I've been crying. (My mother taught me that one—it really works!)

Exercise #2: Now it's your turn.

Since you've seen an example of some ways to make these lists come alive, it's time to give some thought to the things you can do to bring life to your own. It's worth repeating: having the lists is one thing, it's *using* the things you've listed that brings them alive.

Just like the fire drills, it's practice that makes all the difference.

So take a few moments here and make your plan. Consider what you can do on a regular basis to increase the amount of delight you experience every day. You may be surprised at how little it can take to significantly increase your daily delight!

1. What, specifically, are you going to do to make your list of *visual delight generators* useful every day?

2. What, specifically, are you going to do to make your list of *auditory delight generators* useful every day?

3. What, specifically, are you going to do to make your list of *kinesthetic delight generators* useful every day?

Way to Go!! Practice giving yourself the gift of delight, daily, and you will be amazed at the results. After all, you've been giving delight as a gift to all the people that you love for years now. Turnabout is more than fair play. Enjoy Yourself!

Affirmations for "Try Smiling"

* *I am willing to consider smiling, even when I don't feel like it.*

* *I am willing to believe that a smile can improve any experience.*

* *I deserve to smile on a regular basis. I deserve to feel good, in spite of my circumstances. I've got just the plan to do it!*

* *I deserve to enjoy my life. Toward that end, I will start my day with a smile.*

* *I have enough smiles to share with everyone I meet.*

Write your own affirmations below:

Workpage: Try Smiling

Now that you know how to get more smiles in your day, record your experiences. Once you've tried the strategies and exercises in this section, pick a time when you used one and describe what happened. (Feel free to copy this page for your personal use.)

What was the situation:

Here's what I did:

Once I did it, I felt:

Using this strategy resulted in:

The next time I have this opportunity, I will:

The Fourth T: Take Time for *You* Every Day!

This last "T" can pose quite a challenge for some people. When I suggest to my audiences that spending time with yourself can be a powerful stress reducer, I'm often asked, "Could I ask a friend to help me? I don't have to do this alone, do I?"

It seems that, nowadays, the word *alone* means that somebody you didn't want to leave you left you for somebody they liked better. And nobody likes that. Why would anybody want to feel that way on purpose?

Many people don't want to be alone, unless it's with someone special. Those special people are the ones who know us so well that, when we're with them, we don't have to pretend to be anything but ourselves. These are the people who can read our minds, who know all about us and who love us anyway.

When you think about the people you'd include in that special group, is it likely that you count yourself?

If you suddenly had 30 minutes of free time with no pressing obligations, what would you do with it?

Many people tell me that they would do something for a friend. They might call someone they care about to see if they needed anything. If all else failed, they'd probably find some chore to do around the house or in their office.

Let me ask you a question here: What's so scary about being alone with yourself? Do you know something that you're not telling the rest of us? If *you* don't want to be alone with yourself, why would anybody else want to be alone with you?

If this feels like an unkind question, let me assure you that I ask it with love. It's not hard to remember a time when I didn't want to be alone with myself, either. I take the way I behave for granted now, even though my ability to be alone with myself is only about 10 years old.

In fact, my ability to use any of the Four T's began with behaviors that I took pains to practice on a regular basis. None of this was second nature to me then.

So when I ask you why anybody else would want to be alone with you if you don't want to be alone with yourself, I know I'm asking a loaded question.

If you're reading this book, chances are that there is at least one person in the Universe who would love to be alone with you. There's at least one person (and I would bet money that there are many more) who sees all the good in you, no matter what.

Even so, this strategy often requires a little more work than the previous three. I must assure you, though, that despite all the circumstances, the experience that provided the catalyst for discovering this Fourth "T" was one that absolutely changed my life.

In 1977, I was an E-4 in the U.S. Navy. I was stationed in San Diego California, and I was sandblasting and painting submarines on a submarine dry-dock.

I was a Boatswain's Mate (bosun's mate). What's a Boatswain's Mate? Well, you've heard of Popeye? Well, Popeye was a Boatswain's Mate. Spinach and all!

At that point in my life, I had two responses to any circumstance: *fight* or *fly*. There was no doubt in my mind that those two responses would be sufficient to handle any situation, because I knew what kind of a person I really was.

I was despicable.

I learned that word when I was seven years old. I knew it was about me. The first time I ever heard it, this word was being used (right to my face!) to describe me.

Now I might have been despicable, but I was not stupid! Even at that age, I certainly knew how to look up words in the dictionary. That very day, I found that big word in the family dictionary by sounding it out. There it was...

And right next to that word, was a picture of me!

(OK, so I'm kidding. There might just as well have been a picture, though. That's how much I took it to heart.)

In any case, I was effectively convinced that this word was about me. I spent the rest of my life, from age 7 to age 25, proving to everybody, everywhere, just how despicable I was.

By September of 1977, I felt that I had only two choices left...

Suicide...

...or therapy.

(It was obvious to me, even then, that if I wanted to have the opportunity of trying both options, I'd have to be very careful about which one I chose first...)

So I went down to Community Mental Health, handed this woman $25, and told her, "My life's a mess. You fix it!"

Gwen Nichols didn't even bat an eye. She said, "You know, I think we *can* fix it. Here's what I want you to do. I want you to go home, look yourself in the eyes in the mirror for 10 seconds. Do it every day for one week. Then you come back and see me, and we'll get started."

I was stunned.

I'd just given this woman $25 of my hard earned cash, and she was sending me home to look in my eyes in the mirror? It seemed ridiculous.

However, I was painfully aware of the alternative, so I went home and tried it.

In the process, I found a great place to try it, too. It was the bathroom—the one room in the house where I had everything I needed.

It had a door that locked. Now isn't it true that even if no other door in your house locks, the bathroom door *locks?*

It had a trash can to put up against the door. (You know, that can's not really for trash, it's for security!)

It had a light switch, and it had a mirror.

Now that I had checked out the facilities, I prepared myself to complete my assignment.

I went into the bathroom and I locked the door. I put the trash can up against the door. I checked the lock. I repositioned the trash can and I checked that lock one more time.

(For the record: I lived *alone*.)

Now that the security issues were dealt with, I stood around in the bathroom for awhile—stalling.

Shifting my weight from foot to foot, I tried to figure out the best position from which to try this task. After an interminable amount of time, I started a windup—just like in baseball. One. Two. Three.

I looked myself squarely in the face and counted: "onetwothreefourfivesixseveneightnineten!!"

Much to my amazement, lightening did not strike. The ground did not open up and swallow me...

And it only took me six weeks to turn the light on!

Looking back on it, I'm amazed at how easy all this seems to me now.

Today, this experience has turned into a humorous story. It gives me a great ending for my programs. I'm very far removed from the pain I felt while I was living through it. At the time, though, there was very little humor in it.

I mention this because I can see, from the perspective of this distance in time, all the opportunities I've had since I survived this experience. I could never have imagined them at the time. I've been told, too, that most really funny stories are created as the result of working through great difficulties.

This mirror technique I've shared with you is one I've never given up. No matter where I am, wherever there's a mirror, I know I'll find a friend.

Believe me, no matter how long it takes you to get comfortable with looking into your own eyes, I highly recommend it. You may get the kind of results that I, and many others, have gotten. In the process, you may even find that you are never really alone—as long as you have yourself.

Pretty soon, you'll be able to look in any mirror, anywhere, and find that your best friend is looking back at you.

I must mention that there is another benefit to using this mirror technique. As far as I'm concerned, there is Someone Else who is always looking back at me when I look in the mirror.

I first referred to this entity as "a power greater than myself," then "My Higher Power," and often, "my Guardian Angel." I also refer to it as "the God of my understanding." This, I believe, leaves room for all the names I have heard, Christian and Jewish, Buddhist and Native American, as well as all the names that exist.

It has been my experience, and one that I have heard echoed by others, that taking time for yourself every day is one of the best ways to hear your own "still, small voice." It also gives your soul, your spirit, the inner you, a chance to hear the words of the God of *your* understanding.

The time for *you* gives you the opportunity to discover that you are never, ever, really alone. Knowing this has been one of the greatest stress relievers of my life. As I learned in a 12 Step Program all those years ago, it allows me to "Let go, and let God."

When it comes right down to it, the belief that all things happen for a reason and a purpose keeps me going. No matter how "bad" it might seem right now, taking the time to put things in perspective, alone, gives me the strength to keep moving forward.

With all my heart, I wish you the joy of taking time for yourself. Every day.

Taking Time for *YOU* Exercises

When you think about it, isn't there at least one other person in this world who loves you very much and enjoys being alone with you? What is it about you that this person loves? There are a couple of ways to find out.

1. Ask someone who loves you to tell you what it is they love about you. You can do this any way you want to: write a note, make a phone call, visit them in person. You can even ask more than one person! The more people you ask, the more information you'll get. Use what works for you. Record how you feel when you receive the information here, on a separate piece of paper, or in your journal.

2. After you get the information about yourself from your friend(s), record your findings. Get a piece of paper and make two columns. Or you can make two columns in a page of your journal, or you can fill in the space below.

In the first column, write "I Knew It!" and record each quality your friend described that you already knew. In the other column, write "No Kidding?" and list the qualities they described that surprised you.

I Knew It.	No Kidding?!

Once you've finished your lists, set the kitchen timer (or a stopwatch) for 15 minutes. Spend that time thinking/feeling about what you've learned. Record your impressions and/or discoveries.

3. This is an exercise to allow you to practice being alone with yourself. Set the kitchen timer for 10 or 15 minutes and spend that time being alone with yourself, just sitting still in a comfortable place. Notice the feelings that you experience. (boredom? anxiety? relief?) When the timer goes off, write down your thoughts on what you experienced.

4. Take a chance with the bathroom mirror. Try looking in your own eyes in the mirror for 10 seconds. Who's home? (You may be surprised.) No matter what happens, write down your reaction to the experience.

5. Try an experiment. Pick a period of time during which you will try looking in your eyes in the mirror for 10 seconds a day. Try it for a week—then a month. Take a separate sheet of paper to record your experiences, or record them in your journal.

At the end of that week or month, take some time to sit by yourself and consider what you've learned. What have you discovered?

When you learn to spend time with yourself, some amazing things will begin to happen.

You will discover lots of things that are wonderful about you. You might find that it's become much easier, and more enjoyable, to accept compliments. People who take compliments well are much more likely to receive them. Next thing you know, you might even be *giving* compliments on a regular basis! It's amazing how much more beauty there seems to be in the world once we recognize the beauty in ourselves.

More than all of that, spending time with yourself will give you the opportunity to discover what you like and what you don't like about your life. That's the first step in making choices, and changes, for yourself.

Affirmations for "Take Time for You Everyday"

* *I am willing to consider making time for myself.*

* *I am willing to believe that there is enough time for me today.*

* *I deserve to have some time for myself. I will take 15 minutes for myself today and do something that pleases me.*

* *I deserve to take the time to discover my own dreams, desires and goals. I take that time for myself today and enjoy it.*

* *I take time for myself today and every day. The more I give myself, the more I have to share with others. I am blessed with time to spare.*

Write your own affirmations below:

Workpage: Take Time for *You* Everyday

While you're learning the process of spending time with yourself, use these questions to stimulate your thinking about your experiences. (Feel free to make copies of these questions for your personal use.)

What I did with (or for) myself today:

How that felt:

The results of doing this were:

Random thoughts/Comments:

Part Four:

A Cheese Pizza

Epilogue

Some Final Words...and a Story

Congratulations! You now have all the tools you need to start your personal stress management program.

You've seen the biological components of the stress response and you know how your thoughts affect your body's response to any situation.

You know the difference between Primal Brain behavior and Modern Brain behavior.

You know about affirmations. You've read how using affirmations can positively supplement any of the behavior changes you want to make. You may even have started using some of the affirmations in this book and discovered the effects for yourself.

You have the template for the Four Week Plan. You have the ability to get yourself in good physical shape, so that you'll be more likely to use your Modern Brain instead of your Primal Brain.

You understand the Four T's. You have specific strategies to work through stressful situations, as well as templates to develop strategies of your own.

You have everything you need to improve the quality of your life on a daily basis and to reduce the impact of stress. Does this mean that you will have a perfect life from now on?

Hardly. What it *does* mean is that you will have choices.

From now on, you can choose to lift your nose from that grindstone and have some fun—no matter what's going on around you. Taking better care of yourself means that you will increase your ability to find delight all around you.

That, alone, can be a significant stress reducer!

Stress management is—you guessed it!—a process. You get the opportunity to practice your skills in everyday circumstances. It's educational, every step of the way.

And speaking of educational, some of the best education

I've ever had has come from stories. How about you?

Do you have a favorite fairy tale or novel that really speaks to you about the things you care about? I do, too.

That's why, as we finish this book together, I'd like to leave you with a story of my own to put all the things we've explored together into perspective.

With great help from Inspiration, this story has been written especially for you—as you make your way through your own Pizza, and your personal Art of Life Management.

A Faerie Story

Once upon a time, there was a little girl who remembered that she was a Faerie Princess.

She would drape herself in her mother's old sheets and float around the house, practicing being regal. In her mind's eye, those sheets were garments of the finest silk. She could feel, emerging from between her little shoulders, the most beautiful gossamer wings, of the most delicate colors.

She would tie long braids of yarn to her head, remembering that she had hair that flowed down her back past her knees. She'd put flowers in the yarn hair, remembering that her Faerie hair was bound in the brightest of jewels and the whitest of sea pearls. She was a Faerie Princess, after all, and she could have all the jewels in the Universe.

At night she would look at the stars in the sky and wish on the first one she saw. She thought great thoughts, about the world, and her place in it, and all the wonderful things she would do when she grew up and became the Faerie Queen. She loved the fireflies on summer nights, seashells and the sound of the ocean, big fires in winter, and laughing. Most of all, she loved life. If she could, she would have gulped it from a glass.

One day, an evil sorcerer put a very deep, very wide,

very strong spell on the little Princess. As a result, she completely forgot who she was.

Because of this spell, she became convinced that she was merely a mortal girl, and not a very pretty one, at that. She lost her beautiful hair, and the jewels and pearls that bound it. She lost her gossamer wings and her resplendent silken clothes.

All she had to wear were dirty rags that didn't fit. Her hair never grew past her ears, which were always dirty. She never floated anywhere, either. Once the spell had been cast on her, she kept her eyes and head down and never looked at the stars.

While she was still growing up, she went to school and did what she was told. She didn't laugh much.

As she grew older, she simply wandered through her life. She met people, did things, moved, and worked, but she never remembered who she really was.

When she was a quarter of a century old, something mysterious happened.

This was the height of a time during which all she wanted to do was die. She had been so miserable for so long, that she could not imagine living to 30. However, try as she might, she simply could not come up with a decent method of killing herself. There just wasn't anything available that she could manage to use successfully.

One day, in the midst of her distress, she heard about a woman who was helping people to find their true spirits, to align themselves with their purpose in life. She figured that it wasn't possible that she could be one of the people who had a purpose in life. But since she couldn't go on being this miserable and she couldn't figure out a way to end her life, she thought the woman might be able to suggest something that could help her, even if it was just a little.

So she went to see the woman, whose name, by the way,

was Nutmeg. When this girl, who had been a Faerie Princess and had grown up without remembering it, arrived at Nutmeg's door, she was welcomed in graciously by Nutmeg herself. "Come in, young woman," said Nutmeg. "You are welcome here."

At this kindness from Nutmeg, the grown-up girl realized that she was, all of a sudden, uncomfortable. As a matter of fact, she realized that she felt ashamed to be receiving such kindness from a stranger. She thought to herself, "If Nutmeg only knew what an awful, unworthy creature I am, she would never be so nice to me. I don't deserve this."

But she went in anyway.

Once she was inside, Nutmeg offered her a cup of tea, which she took. Then, sure enough, just like she'd heard about, Nutmeg asked her if she'd come about a mirror. Looking down, the grown-up girl said, "If you've got a spare one that nobody's using. Yes, please." At this point, Nutmeg explained to the grown up girl about the mirrors.

These mirrors were created in such a way that whoever looked into one would see their *true self*, no matter what they had seen in other mirrors. No matter what anyone else had told them that they looked like. It just so happened, continued Nutmeg, that no one who had ever looked into one of these mirrors had seen anything less than a beautiful, magical creature, full of Light and Love, looking back at them.

The grown up girl thought to herself, "There's always a first time." And then, ashamed as she was, she looked in the mirror.

At that exact moment, she had the strongest physical sensation she had ever had. It was as if she was being held, like a little baby bird, in the great hands of some Being much larger than her—much larger than the world, even.

She was held so tenderly, so gently, that it almost made her heart break with emotion.

As she looked into the mirror, she saw the most beautiful face that she had ever seen in her entire life. The warmest, gentlest eyes, beautiful skin, a soft smile—and dimples!

She heard, with every fiber of her being, the tenderest, sweetest voice say to her, "You are beautiful. You are good. You are a child of God, and *you are immeasurably loved.*"

For a few moments, the grown-up girl was completely filled with Light. It was the most amazing, healing, peaceful feeling that she had ever known. For those few moments, she was filled with something that can only be described as delight. If she had died right there on the spot, she knew she would die happy.

The grown-up girl did not, however, die.

She lived. And from that day forward, she searched the entire world to find something that would connect her again with that feeling of delight, that feeling of complete peacefulness that she had experienced when she looked in that mirror.

Although she began her search immediately, she did not find it right away. The time she spent searching is of little importance to our story; what matters is that she searched as long as she had to, and never stopped until she found what she sought. It seemed like a long time.

It appeared to her, during the years that she searched, that she had had little success. In truth, though, every single thing she did had a negative affect on the sorcerer's spell.

Bit by bit, it was being dismantled. Bit by bit, it was losing it's power over her.

However, since it was a very strong (and wide, and deep) spell, it took some time for her efforts to show. After awhile, though, it became obvious—even to her—that something was, in fact, changing inside her.

It was not long before she started to take better care of herself. She started to get more rest, she started to pay attention to what she ate (especially breakfast), and she started to walk in the parks around her home. For the first time in a very long time, she noticed how beautiful the trees were, how graceful the birds were that flew overhead, and how in summer—at dusk—there were always fireflies.

The fireflies reminded her of stars, and soon she began to look for them every night. Once or twice, she even wished on the first one she saw.

The beauty of the stars made her sigh with happiness. Looking around, listening to the sounds of a world that was becoming more and more beautiful to her, made her feel so relaxed and peaceful that it was almost like that feeling she had had, looking in that mirror, so long ago.

Breathing slowly and deeply, she found that she could keep that feeling longer, so she began to breathe that way whenever she thought about it.

If the world was becoming more beautiful, so was that grown-up girl. (One day, she even thought she felt the touch of gossamer wings brush by her cheek.)

Over the years, as she continued to grow, she noticed that there were times that she felt completely free of that old sorcerer's spell. She started talking to herself in a gentle, loving way. On the occasions when she did this, she was certain that the old spells had no power over her.

She looked for positive people, places and things in the world. And when she was with them, she had the strongest feeling of delight—just as she had when she looked in the mirror.

She couldn't help smiling when she thought of all the growing up she had done, and how far out of the clutches of the sorcerer's spell she had come.

One day, while she was out with some friends at a pizza parlor, she happened to look into the mirror hung along the wall above their table.

There, looking out at her from that mirror, was the most beautiful Faerie Queen that she had ever seen—or could ever have imagined!

She was breathtakingly beautiful. She had the longest, shiniest hair, the brightest, most sparkling eyes, and a laughing, dimpled(!) face. In her hair, which was bound with ropes of the most opalescent fresh water pearls, she wore jewels that caught the light and flashed with gemfire. Her robes were of the finest silk, with silver stars on the material.

And she had the most magnificent pair of luminous, gossamer wings.

The grown-up girl could not stop looking at the Faerie Queen in the mirror. After a moment, though, the image faded, and was gone. She was again surrounded by her friends, and one of them asked her if she was alright.

"Oh, yes," said the grown-up girl. "Oh, yes."

She decided at that very moment to spend more time with herself, every day, looking in mirrors until she found that Faerie Queen again.

So every day, she did just that.

With all that persistence, it didn't take long for the Faerie Queen to take up residence in that grown-up girl's bathroom mirror. And every day, they spent time with each other. The more time they spent together, the weaker all the parts of the sorcerer's spell became, until pretty soon, it seemed to have disappeared altogether.

Day by day, the grown-up girl began to discover things that she really wanted to do—and she did them. She made new friends, had more experiences, and even (much to her delight!) found that she was one of those people who have a purpose in life. She even discovered that there were people in this world who thought that *she was a delight*.

To her great joy, she met the love of her life. Every day, she continued to build a life of her own choosing, with love to share. And share it she did, with all she met.

One day, years later, as she was looking in her bathroom mirror at the Faerie Queen, she noticed that her own hair seemed very long—heavy even. She put her hand in it and found a cord of fresh-water pearls and jewels—and hair that flowed past her knees.

She glanced at her wrists and noticed the sleeves of a silken robe made of stars; she looked down at her feet and saw that her beautiful clothes reached the floor, spreading out around her over her feet.

She reached over her shoulder and touched them—the most resplendent pair of luminous, gossamer wings!

The girl who had been a Faerie Princess, but had grown up without remembering who she was, had found, much to her delight and astonishment, that she was the Faerie Queen—the most beautiful and good, of all the Universe.

And since she was the Faerie Queen, she could create anything she desired in the Universe.

Couldn't she?

(You Bet!)

Part Five:

Extra Toppings

Extra Toppings

The following section contains information that is no longer an active part of *Stress Arresters*, although the participants in my day-long workshops have found it to be very useful. Some people just like to have extra toppings for their pizza! Like extra toppings for a real pizza, you can decide which of these extras suit your taste.

Bon appetit!

Extra Topping #1:
Symptoms of Excessive Stress

The following information is adapted from a handout that I used in the early Stress Busters *course. The original handout came from the Navy Drug and Alcohol Counselor School, which I attended in 1984. That Navy handout lists credit for the information as adapted from Jere Yates'* Managing Stress.

The symptoms of excessive stress can manifest themselves in any of three ways: physically, emotionally, and behaviorally. These symptoms are your clue that your body is preparing to fight or fly—or that you're at the Exhaustion Stage.

Knowing these symptoms can give you an advantage: as soon as you realize that you are experiencing one of them, you can stop what you're doing and take care of yourself.

Physical Symptoms of Stress

As your body prepares to fight or fly...

1. Muscles tense up; the result:
   headaches
   chronically tight muscles, especially in the face,
       neck and shoulders
   backaches
   shortness of breath, shallow breathing

2. Digestive system shuts down; the result:
   loss of appetite
   upset stomach
   indigestion, heartburn
   diarrhea or constipation
   frequent need to urinate

3. The body's cooling system is activated; the result:
   excessive sweating

4. The reproductive system is disrupted; the result:
   missed menstrual cycles
   excessive premenstrual tension, PMS
   lack of interest in sex
   impotence

Emotional Symptoms of Stress

Fight	Fly	Exhaustion
anxiety	depression	overpowering urge to cry
irritability	boredom	
obsessive thoughts	loss of zest for life	
feeling keyed up	inability to concentrate	
strong emotions for no apparent reason		

Behavioral Symptoms of Stress

Fight	*Fly*
impulsive behavior	startled by small sounds
insomnia	increased smoking
teeth grinding	increased alcohol and drug consumption
increase in caffeine consumption	compulsive eating
excessive nervous energy	increased spending or gambling
constant movement	impulsive laughter, in the face of serious or "bad" news

Extra Topping #2:
Some Job-related Stress Factors

This information has been adapted from another one of the handouts from the Stress Busters *course, which documents results from clinical studies.*

On the job, we must contend with two things: the tasks we are assigned and the people with whom we work. Both of them have stress producing potential. Even so, it's easier to contend with stress on the job if it's not coming from both directions. That is, if we work with people who we like, the stress of the tasks can be eased. If we're doing work that we like, the stress of interacting with people we don't care for can be eased.

195

Check the following list to assess your potential for a stress overload at work.

PEOPLE

Co-workers compete with each other, there's a lack of cooperation.

Your boss, and the management, run the place from "crisis to crisis."

Your relationship with your boss is poor, at best.

Your only sources of information are Rumor Control and Gossip Central.

TASKS

You're not sure what your job is, exactly.

Working fast is a "must."

No one is really sure about your work objectives.

You have no job security.

You have too much work to do in the time allotted (work overload).

You have too little work to do in the time allotted (job phase out).

You have too little or too much responsibility.

You don't have the authority to carry out your responsibilities.

Several things you have to do are in direct conflict with your primary job description.

Extra Topping #3:
Factors Which Increase the Impact of Stress

This section is adapted from another clinical study report from my substance abuse counselor days...

The things which cause us stress are as individual as we are. One person's Waterloo could be handled without batting an eye by someone else. Generally speaking, the triggers to the stress response are either personal or environmental *and* are directly related to your level of concern in the matter.

PERSONAL

The more critical the outcome is to you.

The more unprepared you are .

The less sufficient your physical & mental resources.

The closer you get to accomplishing your goal.

The lower your personal tolerance for stress.

The less you feel in control of the situation.

ENVIRONMENTAL

The longer the stressful circumstances continue.

The greater the number of requirements to which you must adapt.

The more intense the level of conflict, in a conflict-prone environment.

The greater you perceive the consequences of failure.

Extra Topping #4:
The Roots of Sauntering and
the Four Week Plan

The Four Week Plan has its roots in an article I read in a woman's magazine in 1978. The article described the process of learning how to develop a jogging routine. It's been years since my knees could handle the effects of jogging, but I did get several major benefits for my efforts.

The first benefit was the experience of creating a successful jogging plan. I had never been athletic, had always been referred to as "spastic," and had always experienced the humiliation of being the last kid chosen on any team in gym. For me to attempt this was a major undertaking. However, with the instructions I read in this magazine, I, the uncoordinated spastic of the Universe, succeeded in becoming a proficient jogger. For about 2 years, I regularly ran 3 miles in about 30 minutes, with added time for warm up and cool down. It was exhilaratingly—until my knees let me know who was really in charge of the process.

Because I loved the experience of running/jogging, I wanted to do something similar, rather than give it up all together. That's when I started walking regularly. Over the last fifteen years, I've discovered that nothing rejuvenates my spirits better than a brisk walk for an hour or so in beautiful countryside. Wow! It's better than a runner's high!

So my second benefit was a love of walking.

When I was putting together the exercise part of the Four Week Plan, it occurred to me that I had used the very same time line—four weeks!—to develop my plan for getting in better physical shape. It was a direct result of my experience of "becoming" a runner in that four weeks in 1978.

Not only that, I knew that just starting out with a short

walk as the exercise for week number three could give the people who tried it such a feeling of success. That feeling of success could help them to become more inclined to extend their walking time on their own.

Voila! It was the beginning for beginners—just the place where I had started all those years ago.

Just in case you'd like to start your own four week plan of walking/running/jogging, I've included the process I followed. I've written it from memory, since the article is long gone.

Like the Four Week Plan, it's a detailed process, with specific behaviors for each week. Every week, you build on what you've accomplished the previous week. As usual, please be gentle with yourself, and accept the pace that your body sets for you. It's patience and persistence that will make all the difference.

Here's the four week plan for walking, adapted from that article and my own experience.

WEEK #1. This week, you simply walk as far as you can, as comfortably as you can, starting with 15 minutes: 7.5 minutes out, and 7.5 minutes back. "Comfortably" means that you can walk and talk at the same time without gasping for breath. Gasping for breath is your signal to slow down your speed.

On the first day, you only walk for 15 minutes, even if it's just around the block. On the second day, you may find that you walk 20 minutes, or you may walk for 15 again. Your goal is to build up to 30 minutes of comfortable walking by the end of the week. You simply concentrate on the amount of time that you walk, not the distance that you cover.

WEEK #2. This week, you walk for 30 minutes every day, 15 minutes out and 15 minutes back. It doesn't matter how far 30 minutes takes you. It's likely that you will notice an increase in distance you can cover and the ease with which you cover it, but that's a secondary benefit of the process. The goal is simply to walk 30 minutes a day, every day.

WEEK #3. This week, you still go for 30 minutes, and you add 5-10 minutes of walking quickly, or jogging, in the middle of your time. You still pay attention to your breathing; if you are out of breath, or can't talk and walk at the same time, you need to slow down. Your lungs will build up to greater capacity as you continue to give them the opportunity to do so.

Incidentally, Breathing 101 is very useful to do as you're walking, too. You can even begin to work up a rhythm while you're walking: breathing in for several steps, then breathing out for several more steps. It's a great way to focus on the process of breathing and walking. It's much more likely to be relaxing if you're concentrating on your breathing than it would be if you are working through any of the things that stress you!

WEEK #4: This week, you increase the amount of time that you walk quickly, or jog. This is the week that you are ready to increase your stamina and lung capacity. You've probably reached the point where you can easily walk quickly or jog for 10 minutes during your 30 minute walk. Each day during the week, time yourself as you increase your quick-walk time. By the end of the week, you should be able to quick-walk for the entire 30 minutes.

By the way, feel free to add 5 minutes to the beginning of your walk to warm up your leg muscles. Adding 10 minutes to the end of your walk will allow you to slow down gradually instead of just stopping abruptly—your muscles will be *so grateful!*

Incidentally, stretching out your legs, arms, and back before and after your quick walks is critical once you get past week #4. If you want to get in the good habit of stretching beforehand, you can even start doing it with week #1. (Why

didn't I mention this in the beginning? Because it's supposed to be simple, you're supposed to start with *one
thing*...and I wanted that one thing to be walking!)

As usual, feel free to do any of this your own way. What
counts is that it's yours... Long after you've put this book
down and forgotten how to spell my name, everything you
design for yourself will be with you. (Kind of like the way
that this running program has stayed with me.)

Extra Topping #5:
Breathing 102

Breathing 102 is a technique I developed from the yoga
breathing I was learning in the late 1970's. I kept it to myself until I realized that it was extremely useful as a method
of relaxation when I had to go to the dentist! (My dentist
has been known to ask me to share it with patients in the
next room when I'm there getting my teeth cleaned.)

It's also my method of choice when it's time to deeply
relax in the midst of a busy schedule, a hectic day, or simply to get myself in an optimal state for prayer and meditation.

Incidentally, once you get proficient at it, it's an excellent breathing technique to use if you're having trouble fall-
ing asleep, especially if your mind is racing or full of all
those things you didn't manage to accomplish during the
day.

When I began teaching this breathing technique during
my day long stress management classes, the people who
tried it seemed to have one of two very different responses
to it.

The majority of the participants who tried it had very
positive responses to the experience. Some people even
told me afterwards that they had never felt as relaxed in

their entire lives as they did after practicing Breathing 102.
Many people would get so relaxed that anyone would notice positive physical changes in the way they carried themselves. And their smiles! Wow. The room seemed to light
up.

There were even people who relaxed so much that they
promptly fell fast asleep on the floor of the gym where we
held the classes! Nobody bothered them, even if they
snored, and they always woke up in time for the end of
class. Smiling.

The results were so wonderful for so many people that
the part of the day when I taught this became one of my favorites.

Even though it was overwhelmingly positive for a majority of the participants in the workshop, there were some
people, who had a very different response to this technique.

For some reason, when they relaxed this much, they
seemed to be releasing all the negative emotions that they
had held inside for so long. For them, breathing shallowly
and remaining tense were the ways that they had kept themselves from feeling emotional pain. When they started to
relax, everything they had been suppressing seemed to be
released all at once. It was upsetting and occasionally,
frightening, to the people who experienced it.

I mention this because it has been my experience that
Breathing 102 is an extremely powerful relaxation technique. It can be extremely healing and it can occasionally
result in a feeling of being emotionally overwhelmed.

You are the best judge of whether it will be beneficial
for you. Please, *please*, pay attention to your response to it.

If you begin to feel uncomfortable in any way, it simply
means that you may have been suppressing uncomfortable
emotions by breathing shallowly and remaining tense. I
highly recommend discussing your response with a trusted

counselor, minister or friend. Once you work through whatever is causing you the discomfort, you can always try this again. You very likely will have a completely positive experience.

It's important to note here that the more relaxed you get the more *real* you get. You've heard the expression, "what you see is what you get"? If you have been keeping yourself on a very tight rope for a very long time, you may be quite disconcerted about the feelings that you experience as you relax your grip on yourself.

One of the prerequisites of practicing this technique is that you must be in a place where you are safe. That means safe on all levels, including emotionally.

I've been taught, and I have experienced, that the body doesn't lie. Whatever personal feelings you encounter are the ones that are correct for you, *based on your beliefs and experiences.*

Those of us who no longer know what we are feeling are simply undergoing the result of a body disconnected from its brain. Once the body and the brain become connected again, the feelings will come through loud and clear. It's important that you are ready to handle what comes through.

The Four Week Plan is the way to start getting your body and your brain on the same team. The most effective thing you can do for yourself here is to listen to the signals that you're getting from your body.

If Breathing 102 is *not* relaxing for you, go back to Breathing 101. Congratulate yourself on doing a great job of taking care of yourself. Continue to use the strategies in the Four T's for awhile, and feel free to try this again in the future.

Should you decide to continue...

There are a few preliminaries that you need to attend to before you start your practice of Breathing 102.

1. It's most important, especially when you're first learning how to do it, to set aside some specific time and place for your practice.

To begin with, please plan to have 20-30 minutes of uninterrupted time with yourself. It's not important, especially at the beginning, that you use all the time that you've set aside. It's always better to have more time than you need. As you begin to use Breathing 102 on a regular basis, you'll get better at gauging how much time you'll need. Then you'll be more likely to use all the time that you schedule for yourself.

In addition, you'll need to begin your practice in safe surroundings, in a place where you'll be confident that you won't be interrupted. Take the phone off the hook or leave the answering machine on with the volume off. Let significant others who might be affected know of your plan and your desire to be undisturbed. It's critical to spend this time in a place where you feel safe, or it will be very difficult to relax.

2. In order to be most successful in your first practice, please dress in loose, comfortable clothes and find a comfortable place to sit. A comfortable chair or even a big pillow pushed up against the wall is fine. If you're comfortable, then you know you're doing it perfectly.

3. Once you're physically comfortable, and in a place where you feel safe and know that you won't be disturbed, you can begin the process.

As with Breathing 101, *please read the instructions carefully **before** you begin.* If you take the time to give yourself a mental "dry run," you will find that it's much easier to do it during your first practice.

How to do it...

1. Now that you are physically comfortable, start by taking two slow, deep breaths. Each "breath" is composed

of an "IN" and an "OUT." To simplify things in the beginning, let's call the IN breath "IB" and the OUT breath "OB."

The IB (IN breath) should last just as long as the OB (OUT breath). Breathe IN slowly, then OUT slowly. Breathe IN, then OUT. (IB, then OB. IB, then OB.)

2. Now you are ready to take a series of 5 breaths which will be shorter on the IB (IN breath) and longer on the OB (OUT breath). The reason that the OB is longer this time is because breathing OUT, slowly and deeply, is what relaxes you. That's what we're doing here, deeply relaxing.

Breathe IN for a count of three (IB=3) and OUT for a count of six (OB=6). Do this five times.

(If you can stretch that OUT breath to a count of nine, go ahead. Be sure you don't strain—this is supposed to be relaxing...)

3. Once you've completed your 5 breaths, simply feel what you feel like.

Was this difficult for you? Were you able to concentrate? Do you feel foolish? There is no right or wrong answer here, only an assessment of the process.

What's important here is that you don't judge yourself. You simply allow yourself to experience whatever happens. It's another one of those things at which you get progressively better, once you allow yourself to begin at the beginning.

Allow yourself to continue to sit in this relaxed position for as long as you're comfortable. If you should start to feel yourself beginning to fidget, it helps to continue to breathe with slow, long OB's (OUT breaths) and then shorter IB's (IN breaths). Concentrate on your breathing, and allow your body to relax as much as possible.

When you are no longer willing to sit here, or feel that you are finished, it's time to take the next step.

4. Begin your process of coming back to regular breath-

ing *sl-oooow-ly* . This is not a good time to jump up! You may be feeling a little groggy, too, so just take it easy during this next step.

You will be taking a series of five breaths in the exact opposite progression that you took when you took the series of five breaths to relax.

This time, the IB will be longer than the OB. The longer IB's will invigorate you. (It's kind of like the same thing you do when you're driving late at night, feeling drowsy, and you roll down the windows to take those deep breaths of cold air so you can wake up.)

Begin by taking an IB for the count of 3, with an OB for the count of 2.

Then, IB for 4, with OB for 2.

Then, IB for 6, then OB for 3.

Then, IB for 7 or 8, with an OB for 3 or 4.

Then, IB for 8-10, OB for 4-6.

Before opening your eyes, which will very likely be closed, just breath regularly with the IB and the OB the same count.

Whenever you're ready, open your eyes, stretch, and experience yourself in your surroundings. It's just possible that you will have a great big smile on your face!

Sit for a minute or so and feel how your body feels.

Are you relaxed? Do you feel calmer than is usual for you? How do you feel? Pay attention to your answers.

The more you practice this breathing exercise, the easier it will become for you. If you can have your practice in the same place, and sit in the same position every time, you will find that an interesting thing begins to happen.

Even when you're not planning to do this exercise, the position you sit in to do it will serve to relax you after awhile. In addition, the place in which you've chosen to practice will also relax you...*even when you're not doing the exercise!*

You will find that the more you choose to use Breathing 102 on a regular basis, the more easily you will be able to relax in many different circumstances.

Now that you've read through all of the directions, you're ready to begin...

Extra Topping #6:
Some Practice with Guided Imagery—
A Walk Through the Meadow

When I present and facilitate *Stress Arresters* in a workshop of one or two days, I usually end the day with this guided imagery. Over the years I have had people tell me, later, how much they remember the experience, and how positive it was for them.

I first learned this guided imagery in 1984, when I was a Navy Counselor stationed in Jacksonville, Florida. We used it in our group therapy. I was told that it came from the work of Dr. Carl Gustav Jung, who was a contemporary of Sigmund Freud.

Dr. Jung was a Swiss psychiatrist, who was the founder of the system of psychology called "analytical psychology." You've heard the terms Introvert and Extrovert? Those were Dr. Jung's concepts.

Dr. Jung believed that all people possessed an Unconscious—that part of the mind that stores information not readily accessed by the Conscious mind. According to Dr. Jung, there are two kinds of information stored in the Unconscious. In the Personal Unconscious are stored memories and ideas from one's experiences in life; in the Collective Unconscious are stored mental patterns and ideas that are shared by all the people of that culture, and perhaps, all human beings.

Much of Dr. Jung's work concerns this aspect of the

mind. He believed that, as human beings, our most significant task is to achieve harmony between our conscious mind and our Unconscious. Guided imagery is one way of doing just that.

After watching how effective it was to use this guided imagery with our Navy clients during the year that I used it in Jacksonville, I continued to use it for another two years while stationed in Beeville, Texas.

By the time I started my stress workshops in 1988, at Charter Hospital in Corpus Christi, Texas, I was convinced of its healing effect.

I present it to you here in the hope that you will benefit from it as much as my workshop participants and I have over the last twelve years.

Before we start, though, let me explain something about guided imagery.

Guided imagery is attended to by the same part of your brain that attends to fairy tales and bedtime stories. It's the part of the brain referred to by Dr. Jung as the Unconscious. The Unconscious is the most magical part of your brain, the part that gets real meaning from stories and metaphors. It's also the part of your brain where dreams are made.

For some reason, things that you might not consciously accept or understand are accepted and understood by your Unconscious mind when presented in the form of stories and metaphors.

The guided imagery that follows is a kind of "fill in the blanks" metaphor. Its purpose is to allow your Unconscious mind to present to you some information about how precious you are, how good you are, and how much you are loved. Your experience will be unique, because each person has a particular experience that means something only to them.

I can't explain why this is so, I've only seen it work this

way, consistently, over the years. If you practice this
guided imagery more than once, you can repeat the same
experience you had the first time you tried this, or you can
have a different experience. I've had both things happen as
I used this guided imagery over the years.

Now that you've decided to try this...

*As usual, it's a good idea to read through this process
before you try it. Give yourself the benefit of a mental "dry-
run."*

As you begin, spend a few minutes breathing deeply—
Breathing 101 or Breathing 102, whichever is your prefer-
ence. Once you feel relaxed, you can take this guided tour
through your imagination. You can have someone read it to
you, or you can record yourself reading it on tape, then just
play the tape. Whichever way you choose will be perfect—
you can decide the one that's best suited to you.

The tour...

It's spring outside. You are sitting in a field of tall, green
grass. The sky is your favorite color of blue, the sun is
warm on your face, and a slight breeze gently ruffles your
hair. The perfect number of your favorite clouds are in the
sky, the perfect number of your favorite birds are flying
overhead, and you feel completely safe and happy. You
have no appointments or obligations right now. You are
free to enjoy yourself and your surroundings.

Enjoy the sights and smells, the sounds and all the sen-
sations of warmth and peace for a moment.

Once you've finished enjoying the peacefulness of sitting, you decide to take a walk through the grass. This
grass, in your favorite color of green, spreads out in all directions around you. As you stand up, you notice a path
through the grass which heads in the direction of the sun.

You follow the path.

As you follow it, you continue to be completely aware of everything around you. All the sights, smells, sounds, the sensation of your feet hitting the ground, the warmth of the sun—everything.

As you continue to walk, you notice some trees up ahead. You're not surprised to discover that they are your favorite kind of trees. You're completely relaxed and at peace as you keep walking, immersed in your surroundings, knowing that you are safe and free.

As you continue to walk, you notice that the number of trees is increasing and the amount of tall grass is decreasing. As you move further along the path, you realize that you are entering a forest. Notice the difference in the air temperature as you move further into the trees and leave the open meadow behind.

As you continue along the path, you realize that you seem to be traveling at an incline—you are headed *up*. You make your way at a leisurely pace, and you notice that your path is heading off to the right. Following it brings you to a small clearing at what seems to be the top of a hill.

Look around and notice your surroundings here. The clearing is open and circular, the sun is shining through the trees. What else do you see? What else do you hear?

Once you've finished exploring this new place, you notice, over to the right, that there's something that looks like a cave, half-hidden by the trees. As you move closer to investigate, you notice that in front of the cave opening there is a circle of stones. Burning inside the circle a bright, inviting fire crackles. You can feel the fire's warmth as you move closer.

If you look up from the fire, you'll see some movement near the entrance of the cave. If you look closely, you'll see that someone is coming towards you from inside the cave.

This person is smiling, and their arms are extended in

welcome to you. You realize that something about them is very familiar; you discover that this is someone you know! This is someone who loves you very much and whom you love, too. You walk right to them and are embraced in a warm, loving hug. Feel all the warmth and tenderness of that hug. Stay for a few moments in this embrace, and let this feeling of love reach every corner of your heart.

When you've finished that welcoming hug, let yourself be led to sit beside the fire, on a stone or a log or something soft that's been prepared for you. This person who loves you has something special for you, deep in a pocket of their clothes. With a smile, they reach in to get it and pull out a drawstring bag.

Look at the bag for a moment and imagine what it would feel like to touch it—then reach your hands out to accept it from the person who hands it to you with all their love.

Feel the weight, feel the texture of the bag—pay attention to every detail.

Reach inside the bag and pull out your gift.

Look at every detail, every facet of this gift until you understand the significance of what you hold in your hands.

Look at it so intently that you *become* this precious something—and look out into your own face. See the beauty there. Feel what it feels like to be treasured. Listen to the words in your mind. Savor the experience for as long as you like...

When you are finished experiencing this, come back into yourself. You now have the knowledge of what you really are, knowledge that will always be yours. Put your gift back into the drawstring bag, and put it in your pocket. You'll find that it fits perfectly. The gift you have received is yours forever, always in your pocket where you put it.

Look into the face of the person next to you and thank them, in your own way, for the gift they have given you. Listen to what they have to say.

When you are finished, both of you stand up. It's time to say good-bye for now, because you both know that you are free to return here any time. Now that you know the way, you know that you will always find someone here who loves you.

After all the good-bye hugs you need, you head back down the hill. Pay attention to everything you see and hear on the way down. Pay attention to the way you feel as you continue back, knowing what you know, carrying what you carry. Take your time.

As you continue through the trees, you notice that the air is becoming warmer, the grass is becoming thicker and the trees are almost all behind you. Follow the path through the meadow until you find the place where you began this journey.

When you find it, and relax in the grass, you close your eyes to the world around you, and feel the peacefulness in your body and the warmth of the sun on your face.

Whenever you're ready, you can open your eyes. You are back to the chair you are sitting in, the cushions you are lying on, to wherever you were when you first closed your eyes to begin this guided imagery.

Note: Many people have reported that, after completing this exercise, they feel compelled to write down what they have experienced.

If you keep a journal, you're a step ahead. If not, you can always start one. If you're one of those people who write to remember, writing your thoughts down anywhere will serve the purpose.

Whether you record it or not, it will be perfect for you. You can trust yourself.

212

Resources Section

Resources: More Information on the Brain

Richard Bandler, *Using Your Brain for a Change*
Real People Press, Moab, UT. 1985. ISBN: 0-911226-27-3

Judith Hooper & Dick Teresi, *The 3 Pound Universe*
Macmillan Publishing, NY. 1985. ISBN: 0-13-920422-9

Gerald Kushel, *Effective Thinking for Uncommon Success*
AMACOM, New York. 1991. ISBN: 0-8144-5964-1

Richard Restak, M.D., *The Brain*
Bantam Books, NY. 1984. ISBN: 0-553-05047-8

Resources: More Information on Affirmations

Connirae Andreas, Ph.D. & Steve Andreas, M.A., *Heart of the Mind: Engaging Your Inner Power to Change with Neurolinguistic Programming*
Real People Press, Moab, UT. 1989. ISBN:0-911226-31-1

Amy Dean, *Night Light: A Book of Nighttime Meditations*
Hazelden Foundation, M.N. 1986. ISBN: 0-89486-381-9

Louise L. Hay, *You Can Heal Your Life*
Hay House, Santa Monica. 1984. ISBN: 0-937611-01-8

Louise L. Hay with Linda Carwin Tomchin,
The Power is Within You
Hay House, Santa Monica. 1991. ISBN: 1-56170-019-3

Susan Jeffers, Ph.D., *Feel the Fear and Do It Anyway*
Fawcett Columbine, NY. 1987. ISBN: 0-449-90292-7

Rokelle Lerner, *Daily Affirmations for Adult Children*
Health Communications, Deerfield Beach, FL. 1985.
ISBN: 0-932194-27-3

Patricia Remele, *Money Freedom: Finding Your Inner Source of Wealth*. ARE Press, Virginia Beach , VA. 1995. ISBN: 0-87604-333-3

Resources: Information on the Four Week Plan

Harvey and Marilyn Diamond, *Fit For Life*
Warner Books, New York. 1985. ISBN: 0-446-30015-2

Richard Hittleman, *Richard Hittleman's 28 Day Exercise Plan*. Workman Publishing, NY. 1969. ISBN: not listed

Susan Perry & Jim Dawson, *The Secrets Our Body Clocks Reveal*. Rawson Assoc., NY. 1988. ISBN: 0-89256-315-X

Susan Powter, *Stop the Insanity!*
Simon & Schuster, NY. 1993. ISBN: 0-671-79598-8

Mabel Elsworth Todd, *The Hidden You*
Dance Horizons/Exposition Press, New York. 1953. ISBN: 0-87127-096-X

Resources: More Information on the Four T's

Melody Beattie, *Codependent No More*
Hazelden Foundation, MN. 1987. ISBN: 0-06-255446-8

Melody Beattie, *Beyond Codependency*
Harper Hazelden, New York. 1989. ISBN: 0-06-255418

Michael Brooks, *Instant Rapport*
Warner Books, New York. 1989. ISBN: 0-446-39133-6

Albert Ellis, Ph.D. & Robert A. Harper, Ph.D.
A New Guide to Rational Living
Wilshire Book Company, North Hollywood, CA. 1975. ISBN: 0-87980-42-9

Robert A. Johnson, *Inner Work*
Harper & Row, San Francisco. 1986. ISBN: 0-06-250437-1

Robert Lauer, Ph.D. & Jeanette Lauer, Ph.D.,
Watersheds: Mastering Life's Unpredictable Crises
Little Brown & Co., Boston. 1988. ISBN: 0-316-51629-5

Dr. Sidney B. Simon, *Getting Unstuck*
Warner Books, New York. 1988. ISBN: 0-446-39024-0

Resources: Information on Life Management

Anonymous, *Twelve Steps and Twelve Traditions*
Alcoholics Anonymous World Services, New York. 1953.
ISBN: 0-916856-01-1

Ann McGee Cooper, *You Don't Have to Go Home From Work Exhausted*
Bowen & Rogers/Bantam, NY. 1990/2.
ISBN: 0-553-37061-8

Jeff Davidson, *Breathing Space: Living and Working at a Comfortable Pace in a Sped Up Society*
Master Media Limited, NY. 1991. ISBN: 0-942361-32-6

Sharon Faelton, David Diamond & the Editors of Prevention Magazine, *Take Control of Your Life - A Complete Guide to Stress Relief*
Rodale Press, Emmaus, PA. 1988. ISBN: 0-87857-757-2

Peter G. Hanson, M.D., *The Joy of Stress*
Andrews McMeel & Parker, Kansas City. 1986.
ISBN: 0-8362-2412-4

Lucy Hedrick, *Five Days to An Organized Life*
Dell Publishing, New York. 1990. ISBN: not listed

Blair Justice, Ph.D., *Who Gets Sick - How Beliefs, Moods and Thoughts Affect Your Health*
Jeremy P. Tarcher, Inc. LA. 1988. ISBN:0-87477-467-5

Douglas Steward, *How to Stay Stressed**
Inword Press, Santa Fe, NM. 1994. ISBN: 1-56690-325-4

(* It's not a misprint... and it's a great read!)

Resources: Extra Toppings

Emmet Fox, *The Sermon on the Mount: The Key to Success in Life*
Harper & Row, SF,CA. 1966. ISBN: 0-06-062862-6

Emmet Fox, *Power Through Constructive Thinking*
Harper & Row, SF, CA. 1968. ISBN: 0-06-062861-8

Thich Nhat Hanh, *The Blooming of A Lotus: Guided Meditation Exercises for Healing and Transformation*
Beacon Press, Boston. 1993. ISBN: 0-8070-1222-X

Susan Hayward, *A Guide for the Advanced Soul*
In Tune Books, Australia. 1984. ISBN: 0-316-35746-4

Thomas Moore, *The Care of the Soul: A Guide for Cultivating Depth and Sacredness in Everyday Life*
Harper Perennial, New York. 1992.

Gary Zukav, *The Seat of the Soul*
Fireside Books, New York. 1989. 0-671-69507-X

About the Author

Maura Beatty is a professional speaker, trainer and consultant who specializes in teaching people how to communicate more positively with themselves and others. She is the president and owner of Alpha Beatty Communications.

She received her BA in Psychology and Communications from the former Corpus Christi State University (now Texas A&M University at Corpus Christi) in 1989, at the age of 37. She is a veteran of over eleven years in the U.S. Navy.

Maura is active in the National Speakers Association and Meeting Professionals International.

She lives in Austin, Texas, with her husband, Chuck, and her two cats.

For More Information...

If you would like additional information about Maura's programs, or her company, you can write to her at:

Alpha Beatty Communications
8760-A Research Blvd., Ste. 387
Austin, Texas 78758

e-mail: MauraB624@aol.com

Order Form

Stress Arresters

After nine years of presenting to audiences around the country, Maura Beatty brings her dynamic *Stress Arresters* into your home or office. This one hour video takes you on a hilarious and heart-warming trip through Maura's stress baggage. You will laugh as you learn the Four Week Plan for reducing the impact of stress in your life. Maura closes the program with her Four T's—the mental strategies for dealing with stress. Filled with warmth and humor, this program is a wonderful combination of stand-up comedy and a hug from a friend.

Bootstrap Words
(Pull Yourself Up!)

"I couldn't put it down. It appears to be a simple book, but in fact it is a great big book with big, big thoughts that, when read, understood and applied, can take you to great big places."

—W Mitchell, CSP, CPAE
"The Man Who Won't Be Defeated"

Please Send Me:

_____ Copy(ies) of the *Stress Arresters* Video @ $29.95 each + Shipping
_____ Copy(ies) of *Bootstrap Words* @ $9.95 each + Shipping

Name _____

Address _____

City _____ State _____ Zip_____

Day Phone _____

Please send $4.00 Shipping for each item ordered. Texas residents add sales tax.

Mail orders to: Alpha Beatty Communications
8760-A Research Blvd., Ste. 387 • Austin, Texas 78758